Aberdeenshire
COUNCIL

Aberdeenshire Library and Information Service
www.aberdeenshire.gov.uk/libraries
Renewals Hotline 01224 661511

‘Th(

h(

‘Th(
S

‘I kn
th(
resoul
now. (

‘The peo

‘Extortion is

We were as poor at the end of it all as we were at the start.’

GERRY BRADLEY was an IRA operator all of his adult life, from 1970 until the ceasefire in 1994, carrying out shootings, bombings and raids.

BRIAN FEENEY is Head of History at St Mary's University College, Belfast, and is a political commentator and columnist with the *Irish News*. He was an SDLP Belfast city councillor for thirteen years and is the author of *Sinn Féin: A Hundred Turbulent Years, A Pocket History of the Troubles* and co-author of the award-winning *Lost Lives: the story of the men, women and children who died as a result of the Northern Ireland Troubles*.

INSIDER

Gerry Bradley's Life in the IRA

Gerry Bradley with Brian Feeney

THE O'BRIEN PRESS
DUBLIN

First published 2009 by The O'Brien Press Ltd.,
12 Terenure Road East, Rathgar, Dublin 6, Ireland.
Tel: +353 1 4923333; Fax: +353 1 4922777
E-mail: books@obrien.ie
Website: www.obrien.ie
Reprinted 2009.

ISBN: 978-1-84717-075-0

2 3 4 5 6 7 8 9 10
09 10 11 12 13 14 15

Typesetting, editing, layout and design: The O'Brien Press Ltd
Printed and bound by Scandbook AB, Sweden

Picture credits:
Photographs on pages (ii), (iii) and (vii) by Brendan Murphy, Belfast.
Photograph of Unity Flats on page (viii) courtesy of Pacemaker Press International, Belfast.

CONTENTS

DEDICATION

This book is for my mother and father,
who were republicans before it became fashionable;
and for my comrades in the IRA, who died for Irish freedom.
I remember them with pride.

Gerry Bradley

Unity Flats, in the heart of Belfast,
where Gerry Bradley lived

PREFACE

At our first meeting, after he had introduced himself, Gerry 'Whitey' Bradley's opening remark was the almost Socratic statement, 'The only thing I know is that I'm not an informer.' We were meeting in an unlit house in north Belfast, on a dark November evening in 2006. Bradley had contacted me through the *Irish News*, the northern Irish nationalist daily for which I write a column. He had not given the paper his real name and gave as a contact number a pay-as-you-go mobile phone. When I turned up at the address he gave, he was satisfied that he could recognise me from a photograph in the newspaper.

Such precautions are partly the result of twenty-three years active in the IRA, but they are also an indication of the paranoia, dismay and bewilderment induced among republicans by a string of revelations in 2005 and 2006, which showed that senior figures from both wings of the movement, the IRA and Sinn Féin, had been British agents for years. One of the most prominent of them was Denis Donaldson. Like most republicans in Belfast, Bradley had known Donaldson as a senior figure in Sinn Féin. In 2005

Donaldson confessed to acting as a British spy for twenty years. Donaldson had run the Sinn Féin office in Stormont after the Good Friday Agreement and for years before would have been privy to all the party's political plans and strategies. He was shot dead in April 2006. The suspicion was that others too would be uncovered and, indeed, that proved to be the case when, in February 2008, it emerged that one of Gerry Adams's drivers, Roy McShane, had been working for the British for years.

Men and women like Bradley, who had given their lives to the IRA's armed campaign, were shocked, disgusted and depressed by these revelations. They had been risking their lives for years, confident in the belief that the republican leadership, though they made mistakes, were immune from British influence and were directing the struggle against the British presence in Ireland with the purest of motives. By the early years of this century, no one could be sure of any of that. Of course, Gerry Bradley knew there had always been informers and was always wary of that prospect, but to hear that people at the very heart of the republican movement had been acting as British agents was profoundly unsettling. It led many IRA members to question what they had been ordered to do during the campaign, why they had been doing it and who exactly had wanted it done.

Bradley himself had twice been the victim of informers, spending years interned on the first occasion and months remanded in custody on the second. However, the stream of informers being exposed in high places in the republican movement, coupled with the ready accommodation with Ian Paisley's DUP at Stormont, prompted IRA men, like Bradley, to reassess what had been going on at the top of the movement while they were risking their lives right up until the moment of the 1994 ceasefire.

Bradley wanted to explain his role and motivation in the IRA's campaign and, by extension, that of colleagues like himself, whom he classes as 'operators' – the men and women at the sharp end who did the shooting and bombing from 1970 to 1994. Apart from two periods of internment, in 1972 and 1973-75, and being remanded in custody in 1982, Bradley was active for the whole of that period.

Bradley's main 'theatre of operations' was initially north Belfast, though from the mid-1980s he was a member of an IRA squad that operated in west Belfast as well, and by the early 1990s he had moved into a different IRA role that took him all over the North.

North Belfast was where the 'Troubles' were at their most viciously sectarian. Even years after the Troubles were 'officially' over, in the sense that the major republican and loyalist groups had called ceasefires, interface fences continued to be built in north Belfast to prevent daily exchanges of stones, bottles and other missiles, and sporadic hand-to-hand fighting between youths from loyalist and republican neighbourhoods; 'recreational rioting' the police came to call this behaviour, because of its futility.

During the Troubles, 566 people were killed in north Belfast, about 15 percent of all the deaths in the conflict. Over four hundred of those killed were civilians, many the victims of sectarian murder. Yet the description 'north Belfast' is too wide for the location of the killings and belies the intensity of the conflict. The vast majority of those deaths occurred in an area of about five square kilometres of inner-city north Belfast, comprising districts whose names became well known throughout Ireland and further afield as they featured regularly in news bulletins over thirty years: Ardoyne, New Lodge, Tiger Bay, Unity Flats.

The defining feature of north Belfast is that it is a patchwork of districts, republican and loyalist, each immediately juxtaposed with a district of the opposite persuasion. Thus, republican New Lodge faces loyalist Tiger Bay; republican Ardoyne faces loyalist Woodvale and Crumlin; republican Unity Flats (now gone) faced the loyalist Shankill. The main roads running between these districts, such as the Cliftonville Road and Crumlin Road, were hunting grounds for loyalist murder gangs, the most notorious of which was the Shankill Butchers of the 1970s. Random loyalist killings would be met with IRA retaliation in the form of bomb attacks on loyalist bars and drinking clubs and, particularly in 1976, sectarian shootings which, in turn, would provoke the response of further random sectarian murders and so on.

In the midst of the continuous sectarian conflict in north Belfast, the IRA also waged its campaign against the British army and Royal Ulster Constabulary (RUC), attacking British army and police patrols with gunfire and bombs, and bombing police and army barracks, of which there were many in north Belfast, as well as 'economic' targets such as shops, warehou

These were Gerry Bradley's 'operations'.

From the very beginning of the Troubles, in 19̄

ley played an active role on the republican side. Altho

young, officially, to become a full IRA member until 1971, he wa

fully involved in the daily confrontations that began in the summer

of 1969 between Unity Flats, where he lived, and the fiercely loyal-

ist Shankill. Initially, he was propelled spontaneously into the con-

flict to defend his district from the combined loyalist and police

onslaught in August 1969. Very quickly thereafter, like hundreds

of other teenagers in working-class nationalist parts of Belfast, he

served an apprenticeship of rioting against police and British army,

then in 1971 he joined the IRA, which had quickly established

itself as the defence organisation of his district.

Bradley became a fully-fledged IRA volunteer in the summer of

1971. From then on, apart from the years he spent interned or on

remand, he was engaged for the next twenty-three years almost

continuously in shootings, bombings, bank robberies and other

similar activities on behalf of the IRA. In the early years, he was

central to the IRA's operations in north Belfast. By autumn 1972,

he was Officer Commanding G company, based in Unity Flats.

The following year, he was appointed Officer Commanding the

third battalion of the Belfast Brigade, which covered the whole of

north Belfast as well as nationalist enclaves in south and east Bel-

fast. He was the youngest battalion commander in the IRA. Each

time he was released from custody – 1972, 1975 and 1982 – he joined the IRA and carried on as before, until 1994. Few others stayed on 'active service' so long.

This book sets out to place Gerry Bradley's IRA career in context. It is not simply a list of shootings and bombings in which he engaged. That would be tedious, apart from the fact that he can no longer remember all of the scores of incidents in which he was involved – no surprise, given that in 1972 and 1973 his company could have been involved in three or four operations in a single day. What the book shows is how circumstances changed over the years as the conflict went through different phases, and the tactics and strategy that the IRA as well as the British government and security forces developed to meet those changing circumstances: from the veritable insurrection of the early seventies, with hundreds of men and women in the Belfast IRA, to the late eighties, as the campaign was being run down and IRA operations were carried out by a surprisingly small number of operators like Gerry Bradley. There were about twenty top operators in Belfast by the end of the eighties, actually carrying out shootings and bombings, though there were many more active behind the scenes.

It was Bradley who asked for the book to be written and, as far as possible, it is written in his words. This book is the first about the Troubles to offer an account by an IRA operator that has not been sanctioned or cleared by the republican leadership. Bradley wanted to explain the rationale for his actions and provide a critical insight into the day-to-day workings of the Belfast IRA. Some of the revelations about the incompetence and complacency in the Belfast

IRA leadership are inconvenient truths for the republican movement. There are also uncomfortable truths about the haphazard and lackadaisical way certain operations were planned.

As for Bradley's motives, he has had plenty of time to think about them. His convictions remain those of a simple, traditional republican. 'Born a rebel, die a rebel', sums up his attitude, he says. Indeed, he wanted that to be the title of the book, but such a title might have implied he wanted to continue the military campaign against the British army. He does not. 'The war is over and there's little support for starting it again. Guys who want to start it again – what are they going to do different from what we did and why do they think they'll do it any better?'

His shorthand phrase sums up his adherence to Wolfe Tone's objective: 'to break the connection with England, the never failing source of all our political evils, and to assert the independence of my country'. After his initial unthinking, automatic reflex of throwing himself into the defence of his community as a fifteen-year-old in 1969, it took Bradley some time to learn anything about republicanism. He quickly became convinced, from the evidence of his own eyes, that there could never be any hope of equal treatment for Catholics or nationalists in the North as long as the British government remained in control of any part of Ireland. The only way to obtain equality was to drive them out and achieve Irish unity. That meant fighting the British army, who defended the presence of the British administration in the North. In the 1970s, he strongly believed that was possible.

As time went on, however, it became clear that things were not so simple. Bradley came to realise that the weaponry and manpower the unionist community had at their disposal, in the shape of the RUC and UDR, meant that even if the British army were to leave there would be no victory. Yet, for Bradley, the stronger the IRA was and the more powerful its campaign, the better the negotiating position republicans would have when it came to the negotiating table, as it inevitably would. He remains firmly convinced that it was the IRA that forced the British government to make concessions like the 1985 Anglo-Irish Agreement, and that it was the IRA bombing campaign in England that led the British to begin secret talks with the IRA in 1992.

Equally, he deplores 'the politicians' in the republican movement, whom he calls 'the Shinners' (Sinn Féiners), who settled for too little. Bradley says he is 'army'. He has no time for 'the Shinners', many of whom he regards as free-loading on the IRA's achievements. While he acknowledges there was overlap between IRA and Sinn Féin members, especially towards the end of the campaign, he still draws a sharp distinction between 'army' and 'politicians'. As an example, he relates the exchange between himself and a loyalist prisoner in jail. 'This loyalist was gloating about a rocket attack on the Sinn Féin centre in Ardoyne and how it must have got republicans really worried. I said: "What's that got to do with me? Doesn't affect me. I'm army. That was a Sinn Féin place." It kinda let the air out of his balloon a bit.'

For Bradley, being an IRA volunteer, in the army, legitimised all his actions and he did some terrible things – but everything he did was for 'the cause'. The army was always right. It would be easy to be censorious about his activities, but this book takes the same position as that of Orlando Figes in his monumental work *The Whisperers*, which deals with life under Stalin. Figes interviewed people whose families were ruined but who still believed in 'Stalin's justice', people who did terrible things – informed on relatives and led a double life – and whose own life was destroyed by Stalin. Their lives were deformed by the times they lived through, but their stories have to be told and their motivation explained. Who can say they would not have taken that direction had they lived in the same circumstances?

What particularly galls Gerry Bradley is that he continued to follow the same direction throughout his adult life – giving his all for the republican movement. Every time he asked for reassurance that the campaign was going on, not being run down, that he was not wasting his time, risking his life for nothing, he was told, categorically, that the role of the IRA was crucial. It was years after the 1994 ceasefire that he discovered, like hundreds of others, that the opposite was the case, that the leadership of the republican movement had changed direction, and men and women like Bradley were used until the bitter end of the campaign as a lever to exact every last drop from the British government.

By that time, in the early 1990s, the IRA's military campaign had dwindled to being a tactic, not the motor force it had previously been in the republican movement. Once the tactic was discarded, men like Gerry Bradley were surplus to requirements. They had served their purpose. Finally, in 2005, the IRA was stood down and its surviving members were left high and dry, with no jobs and no prospects.

I

BAPTISM OF FIRE

Bradley vividly recalls the feeling of shock and dismay he shared with all the other onlookers when they saw that the van was carrying pick-axe handles. The IRA had no guns to hand out.

Unity Flats was an estate of social housing near the centre of Belfast whose frontage stretched 350 metres from the bottom of the Shankill Road to Clifton Street. British soldiers knew the district as a hotbed of IRA support. For the soldiers, the flats were a concrete maze of stairways, connecting galleries – or balconies, as the residents called them – dead-ends and dangerous open spaces overlooked by a score of firing positions. Soldiers could be shot at from windows, galleries, doorways, from 'wash-houses' built of lattice-work brick, where washing often hung at the end of each row of flats, or from the flat roofs of the housing complex. Blast bombs, concrete blocks, bottles, bricks or pieces of metal could be hurled from the galleries as soldiers sought cover to avoid the open ground between blocks of flats. Troops always entered the complex in strength, covering each other and trying to move about quickly and unpredictably. In the 1970s, merely driving past Unity Flats in an army Land Rover often invited a fusillade of shots.

The flats had been built to replace nineteenth-century slum housing in the district known as Carrick Hill, where 1,314 tiny houses had sat on thirty-one acres. The area was designated a redevelopment area in 1958 but after the inevitable public inquiry and other delays, clearance did not begin until 1963. The first new home was ready for occupation in May 1967.

When the modern IRA was established in 1970, there were two hundred dwellings in the Unity Flats complex, a classic 1960s development of twenty blocks of medium-rise flats and two-storey maisonettes. Ultimately, Unity Flats would have 315 dwellings, but further planned expansion had been aborted by the outbreak of civil strife in 1969, which led to repeated attacks from the nearby ultra-Unionist Shankill Road, whose residents had always strongly objected to the new complex rising on their doorstep.

How and why did such a small district produce a large number of men and women prepared to risk their lives, to kill, to shoot and bomb, to go to jail for lengthy periods? Why would people living in brand new modern housing become embroiled in such activities? What circumstances changed their lives from a humdrum daily existence in summer 1969 to a frenetic, lethal, high-octane, cat-and-mouse conflict six months later? What did they think they were doing and why?

Some people claim that the name of the development, Unity

Flats, was chosen to symbolise the uniting of two communities, Catholic Carrick Hill and Protestant Shankill, which had been at loggerheads for generations. Others say the name came from Unity Street, which originally ran through the Carrick Hill district. Whatever about aspirations to unite the two communities, the fact is that Carrick Hill was mainly Catholic and it was families from Carrick Hill who had been temporarily cleared out so that the new flats could be built. Since that was so, it would be the same Catholic families who would be rehoused in Unity Flats as each phase was completed. There were never more than a couple of dozen Protestant families living in Unity, and after the August 1969 disturbances, twenty of them moved out. By February 1970, only two Protestant families remained.

In 1969, the blocks of Unity Flats constructed to that date formed a rough quadrilateral, with a dent in one corner where it abutted onto the Shankill at Peter's Hill. The base of the quadrilateral, Upper Library Street, 350 metres long, ran from the Shankill Road to Clifton Street. The narrowest side, facing Peter's Hill at the bottom of the Shankill Road, was 60 metres long. The 'safest' side, because it faced the nationalist New Lodge district along Clifton Street, was 200 metres long. The most dangerous side, the 'front line' so to speak, because it faced the Shankill district across waste ground cleared of slum housing, stretched for a hazardous 400 metres.

This large expanse of waste ground lay ready for the next phase of building. Beyond it stood several streets of partially demolished and derelict housing, the western edge of the nineteenth-century slums of Carrick Hill cleared of their inhabitants. This scene of dilapidation would become a battleground throughout the 1970s between attackers from the Shankill and the new residents of Unity Flats. The empty houses and waste ground provided abundant ready-to-hand missiles: stones, broken bricks, ironmongery and other debris strewn thick on the ground.

By dint of hoisting the people into two- and three-storey flats, modern housing design in the 1960s enabled planners to cram over a thousand men, women and children into an area of less than nine acres, which became Unity Flats. The building materials used in the flats were cheap: the walls were prefabricated and prone to penetrating damp; the roofs were flat, thereby saving the cost of the joists and rafters and tiles that pitched roofs required, but guaranteeing leaks in Belfast's damp, drizzly weather. In a few years, blocked internal downspouts from the roofs would cause great patches of damp on inside walls and drips from ceilings.

Nevertheless, the new homes had modern electrical wiring, heating, toilets and bathrooms, and hot and cold running water in purpose-built kitchens, none of which the people in the nearby Shankill had. Who was to know that the flats would be so horrible to live in and would start to fall apart in less than a decade? They were spanking new and brightly painted, and as more and more of them were completed and the residents moved in, it looked as if block after block of Unity Flats, with its growing Catholic population, was marching up into the Shankill, while there was no sign of any new houses for Protestants.

As soon as the first residents moved into their new homes in 1967, they were attacked. The most vulnerable flats were those called Unity Walk, fronting the Shankill Road at Peter's Hill. Weekends were worst. Supporters of Linfield football club, the North of Ireland's most aggressively Protestant team, would throw bottles and stones and metal bolts at the flats as they returned from matches on a Saturday. On Friday and Saturday nights, drink-fuelled groups of Shankill Road men walking home from the city centre and others emerging from the nearby Naval Club, used Unity Walk for target practice, and intimidated and sometimes assaulted residents foolhardy enough to be in the open.

Paddy Kennedy, the Republican Labour MP for the district, raised the matter of these attacks in the Stormont parliament in March 1969. Windows were broken so often in flats facing the Shankill Road that people gave up replacing them and left them boarded up, he reported. He said that although the numbers of Linfield supporters coming along the Shankill Road were large enough to constitute unlawful assemblies, and that drunks coming from the Naval Club were regularly committing offences, there was no police protection afforded to the people in Unity.

All this was a small foretaste of what was to come. The frequency and ferocity of attacks on the flats increased in direct proportion to the rise in tension across Northern Ireland in 1969. Unionists, gen-erally, had been aggrieved by the demands of the Northern Ireland Civil Rights Association, its controversial marches, and the pres-sure the British government at Westminster was exerting on

Stormont to bring in reforms in voting and housing that would benefit the North's Catholic population – exactly the sort of people who were living in newly-built accommodation in Unity Flats.

As 1969 began, a snap Stormont election was called for February, leading to a bitterly sectarian campaign in which Reverend Ian Paisley played a major role. In March, there was a startling Ulster Volunteer Force (UVF) bombing campaign at reservoirs, which the UVF did not admit and which most unionists therefore believed was the work of the IRA. Water supplies to Belfast and County Down were disrupted. In April, the Stormont Prime Minister Terence O'Neill resigned, as he later said, 'literally blown out of office by the UVF'.

Unity Flats provided a readily available focus for the resentments of anti-Catholic gangs from the Shankill. These fears and resentments of people on the Shankill Road were channelled into aggression by the activities and speeches of local leaders, including the Stormont MP Johnny McQuade, a coarse, foul-mouthed, barely literate former British soldier, ex-boxer and ex-docker.

Most sinister was John McKeague. McKeague was a paedophile whose sexual proclivities had come to the notice of the police. In 1970, he was one of those charged with the 1969 waterworks bombings but acquitted, though in later years he bragged about his involvement. He was rabidly anti-Catholic, a dangerous rabble-rouser who formed the Shankill Defence Association (SDA) in 1969, a body that would play a violent role in the events of August 1969, and in 1971 merged with the murderous Ulster Defence

Association (UDA), responsible for the deaths of 431 people over the period of the troubles. In 1969, the SDA was about three hundred strong. McKeague would go on to found the Red Hand Commando in 1972, a small group of killers linked to the UVF.

Matters came to a head for Unity Flats in the summer of 1969 as the Orange 'marching season' gathered steam. There are two distinct and contrasting views of what happened in July and August 1969. One is the experience of the people living in Unity Flats. The other is provided by the Scarman Report, a judicial inquiry into the disturbances in Northern Ireland in 1969 by Mr Justice Leslie Scarman, a senior English High Court judge.

Here, first, is a condensed version of the official account of events, relying heavily on the Scarman Report.

There had been minor disturbances on the evening of 12 July as Orange bands returned towards the Shankill from the main gathering of Orangemen at 'the Field', as they called it, in south Belfast. To reach the Shankill, they had to pass Unity Flats. There was an exchange of missiles between crowds lining the Shankill Road to watch the marchers and bands and residents of Unity Flats, annoyed by twenty-four hours of noise and provocation, which began in the afternoon of 11 July. At one point, a section of the Orange crowd tried to gain entry to Unity Flats, but were repulsed by a small group of police who had taken up position at the Peter's Hill entrance to the complex. It was pretty much par for the course on 'the Twelfth', the biggest day in the Orange calendar.

Three weeks later, a minor Orange parade, which at worst

should have produced a repetition of the events of 12 July, with cat-calls and minor stone-throwing, instead unexpectedly exploded into intense violence involving hundreds of rioters, and changed the lives of people in Unity Flats forever.

On Saturday, 2 August, a Junior Orange procession was due to parade along the Shankill into the city centre to catch the train to Bangor, a seaside resort on the north County Down coast. Long before the parade was due, crowds from the Shankill had filled the footpath opposite Unity Flats. Ostensibly, they were there to ensure safe passage for the children in the Junior Orange march. In fact, as the Scarman Tribunal found, many of the people assembled at Unity did not comprise an ordinary crowd. John McKeague and his Shankill Defence Association, 200-300 strong, had marched down the Shankill and taken up position on both sides of the road at Unity Flats. They were intent on trouble.

As soon as the parade passed, McKeague's men, led by an individual carrying a Union Jack, launched an attack into Unity Flats. They were held off by the residents in serious hand-to-hand fighting, though several attackers did manage to get into the forecourt of the complex. Altogether, there seems to have been about a dozen policemen on duty at the entrances to the flats from the Shankill end. Residents later accused these policemen of joining in the attack with McKeague's men. Sporadic fighting went on for most of the afternoon until about 4.30pm.

A dangerous rumour then circulated in the Shankill Road that the Junior Orange parade had been attacked on its way into Belfast past Unity Flats. As a result, crowds of people poured down the Shankill to wait for the parade's return, expected some time before 7.00pm. An hour before the expected arrival of the Junior Orangemen, a huge crowd, estimated by the police to be upwards of three thousand, had filled the road at Unity Flats. Shortly after 6.00pm the crowd began to attack Unity Walk, but were repelled by police, who were now present in numbers. The attackers vented their frustration on the flats in what the Scarman Report described as 'a continuous barrage' of stones and other missiles, breaking every window facing Peter's Hill. Others attacked the flats complex from the rear, across the waste ground from the lower Shankill Road and managed to gain access to the courtyards between the blocks of flats, where desperate fighting took place.

There was a real danger that the flats might be overrun and burnt by the Shankill crowd. In the course of the fighting, several residents were batoned by police, and one, sixty-one-year-old Patrick Corry, subsequently died from his injuries, namely three skull fractures. Fighting between police and residents, and between residents and would-be attackers advancing across the waste ground, continued for hours. It was only about 3.00am on 3 August, after police reinforcements had pushed the Shankill crowd away from Unity Flats, that quiet returned.

Yet, later that morning, Sunday, 3 August, a mob of 400-500 appeared again on Peter's Hill opposite Unity Walk. This time there were 200 police with an armoured car and they dispersed the mob, only for them to regroup further up the Shankill and march back down again, led by McKeague's SDA behind a Union Jack. The confrontation then became very serious and continued all day. The mob threw petrol bombs at the police and erected barricades which the armoured car easily broke through, but then gelignite bombs were thrown at the police. Finally, around 1.00am, the police managed to disperse the crowd after several baton charges.

The Scarman Report records that the Belfast Police Commissioner, at 4.45pm on Sunday, had asked for British army troops to be deployed since all police reserves had been committed. The commanding officer of the regiment in question, the Queen's Regiment, consulted Brigade HQ in Northern Ireland only to be told by the chief of staff that committing troops was a political decision that could not be taken without approval from England. Responsibility for British troops was a matter for the British Secretary of State for Defence at Westminster, not the Stormont administration.

In any case, the RUC Inspector-General did not support the Commissioner's request, partly, as he told Scarman, because of 'the political angle that there were constitutional issues involved'. Nevertheless, the point is that a fortnight before the calamitous events in Derry and west Belfast which necessitated troops intervening, the circumstances on the ground between the Shankill and Unity Flats were so serious that senior figures were considering using troops, with all the implications that decision brought with it.

The residents' perspective of the events of 2–4 August was entirely different from the measured tones of the Scarman Report, and the details differ markedly from the official version of events. To them, the inability of the police to protect them from the Shankill mobs was unforgivable, but not accidental. There was no question in the minds of the residents that the police and the invading mob from the Shankill formed common cause. Indeed, there are some passages in the Scarman Report itself that unintentionally support their view. Some instances of collusion between police and John McKeague's SDA are recorded without comment or explanation in the Scarman Report, although Scarman roundly condemned McKeague elsewhere in his report. For example, Scarman did not seem to think the following incident incongruous:

> Some of the Protestants managed to get into the courtyard [of Unity Flats] and fighting broke out between them and the residents. Mr McKeague was present in Upper Library Street during the incident. Evidence was given that he pointed out to the police a youth within the flats who was then set upon by Mr McKeague's supporters and ultimately arrested by the police. (Par 9.6).

Why were police following any directions from McKeague? Why was McKeague allowed to be in Upper Library Street apparently directing operations? Why was he not arrested himself as, evidently, the instigator of the assault on Unity Flats and, indeed, on the particular youth in question here?

It seems that Mr Justice Scarman displayed many of the besetting sins of English judges appointed to enquire into matters in Northern Ireland. He could not imagine that in the RUC he was dealing with a partisan paramilitary unionist militia rather than with a civil police service on the English model. He could not contemplate the prospect that the police might, in fact, have taken sides against the beleaguered residents of Unity Flats. He could not accept that policemen joined the Shankill mob in throwing stones at people in Unity Flats. In short, Scarman tended to believe the police account of each incident.

As a result, he rejected the testimony of Unity Flats residents, sometimes without giving a reason. Mrs Austin, a woman who owned two shops in Unity Walk, testified that a number of police threw stones at the flats. She was even able to identify policemen involved. Scarman says: 'After a full consideration of the evidence, we have come to the conclusion that [the police] did not throw stones. Mrs Austin was mistaken.' But how could she have been mistaken? The police were in uniform, easily distinguishable from the mob. How could she have imagined the incident? Why would she make such an allegation? Scarman concludes, strangely, 'had police been present in sufficient numbers to suppress Protestant stone-throwing, it is likely that the accusation would never have been made.'

Interestingly, when examining events in Derry ten days later on 12 August, Scarman did accept the testimony of Harold Jackson of the *Guardian* newspaper that the police did throw stones and also encouraged Protestant rioters to throw stones at people in the Bogside. The reason the judge accepted the evidence of an English journalist in one case, but rejected that of a respectable businesswoman in another, can only be guessed at. Perhaps the televised pictures of RUC men throwing stones at Rossville Flats left him with no alternative.

Scarman never seemed to have wondered why it was that the only person who died as a consequence of the attacks on Unity Flats was a resident batoned by the police, or why so many people injured or arrested, or both, on 2 August seemed to be Unity Flats residents.

Scarman's general conclusion about the events (par. 9.57) was that

> The riots of 2 and 3 August were begun and continued by Protestant crowds. They led to loss of life and serious damage to property. They were directed initially against Unity Flats but soon developed into a conflict with police. They provide evidence not only of the risk to the peace of the province from Protestant violence but also of the determination of the police to protect Catholic lives and property. Although unable to prevent external damage such as the breaking of windows and on occasions became embroiled (once with tragic results) with the residents of Unity Flats, the police did successfully protect the residents from invasion by Protestant mobs.

The people of Unity Flats regarded the second part of this conclusion as a travesty. For them the events of 2–4 August 1969 were terrifying and life-threatening, and unforgettable in their horror. They were 'besieged', in Scarman's words, by 'a vast crowd'. Repeated assaults on Unity Flats from a number of directions by hundreds of men and youths from the Shankill and by baton-wielding RUC men were repulsed only by desperate defence from the men, and even boys, of Unity Flats. It was 'all hands to the pumps'. Women and children too pelted the invaders from the balconies with anything they could lay their hands on. Able-bodied men used any weapons they could find to prevent attackers getting past the entrances to the flats complex and gaining access to the courtyard, and thence the stairwells. No one was in any doubt that if they had managed to get into the complex, the mob was fully prepared to wreck the place and would have burnt the flats.

One of those on the balconies on 2 August, throwing anything that came to hand, was fifteen-year-old Gerry 'Whitey' Bradley (Whitey, because of his fair hair). His mother prevented him from going down into the thick of the fighting for fear of him being injured. From his vantage point, Bradley saw thousands massing from the Shankill and city centre, accompanied by bandsmen marking time, fifing and drumming incessantly. The noise was terrific. The Shankill crowd had come prepared, with bottles, stones, rivets and bolts, which were soon flying through the windows of Unity Walk and littering the balconies. He watched, in disbelief and horror, the RUC in riot gear leading what he calls 'the Orangemen' in towards Unity. He watched his neighbours beat them back onto the Shankill where they re-grouped, bands still drumming and flutes playing, the roar of the crowd tumultuous.

One of those leading the defence was Emmanuel O'Rourke, a former British soldier who had served in Aden. Bradley can still picture clearly in his mind, as if in a film, O'Rourke fighting police armed with batons. At one stage, he was taking on four policemen who had obviously identified him as a leader, or certainly someone to be reckoned with. In the struggle, they had ripped his shirt off. Eventually they overcame him and batoned him to the ground. He was then dragged across broken glass and other debris and slung into a police Land Rover. His sister rushed, screaming, down from her balcony to his assistance, and was arrested for kicking a policeman.

A rumour swept around Unity Flats that the IRA from west Belfast were coming – and bringing guns. Gerry Bradley remembers seeing a van arriving around 'tea-time' (6.00pm), with Jim Sullivan, a prominent IRA man from west Belfast, in it. Everyone was convinced it contained the guns, and people ran down to watch as the back doors of the van were opened. Bradley vividly recalls the feeling of shock and dismay he shared with all the other onlookers when they saw that the van was carrying pick-axe handles. The IRA had no guns to hand out. The truth was, the IRA was a spent force, its aims in 1969 political rather than military. About forty men managed to make their way into Unity Flats during the afternoon to lend a hand, not as an organised body, but in groups of three and four. Apart from them, the people of Unity Flats were on their own. That weekend a group of men in the flats formed the Unity Flats Association to organise the defence of the district. They were correct in their assumption that the onslaught of 2–4 August was merely the prelude of more to come.

A fortnight later, the North of Ireland exploded in a paroxysm of violence. There was serious rioting in Derry and Belfast and in half a dozen other, smaller, nationalist towns. In west and north Belfast, police opened fire with heavy machine guns mounted on the turrets of armoured cars. Unionist mobs descended on nationalist districts in Belfast, burning houses and displacing hundreds of people. Scarman concluded that 82 percent of those displaced in Belfast were Catholic families. By 15 August, contingents of the British army were on the streets of Belfast and Derry where Catholic communities had thrown up barricades to keep out marauding unionist gangs.

2

THE GENESIS OF G COMPANY

'I loved rioting. So did my mates.
We used to travel to Ardoyne or Ballymurphy.
Six, eight or ten of us would get taxis to the "Murph".
The Murph was the best. There'd be hundreds and hundreds rioting.
It was the real thing: CS gas, British army "snatch squads".
If they caught you, you were in for a pasting.'

The events of August 1969 transformed Gerry Bradley's life and that of thousands of others across the North. For the remainder of 1969, Bradley's time was consumed with the defence of his district, Unity Flats. As 1970 wore on, however, he was champing at the bit to be allowed to participate in the offensive that the newly formed Provisional IRA was mounting against the police and the British army, but, too young to join the IRA, he had to be content with attacking the police and army with stones and bottles: rioting, the Belfast teenager's pastime in the early seventies.

By the summer of 1970 what came to be known as 'the

honeymoon period' for the British army was over. The first IRA bombs had exploded in spring 1970, and in August the first policemen were killed. The Catholic community no longer regarded British soldiers as their protectors, but as the aggressors and occupiers acting at the behest of the unionist regime at Stormont, constantly searching homes and assaulting and insulting the population.

Initially, in 1969, one central determination motivated the defenders of Unity Flats: never again. The Unity Flats Association, formed on the night of the first major assault on the flats on 2 August 1969, immediately began organising the men and boys of the complex to defend the district. In that respect, Unity Flats was a fortnight ahead of other districts, which faced onslaughts from unionist mobs on 14–15 August. The two main figures in the Association, Patsy 'Skin' Burns and William Largey, soon found that the other nationalist districts of Belfast, attacked later in August, also formed defence groups; these would become the nuclei for the emerging IRA. These groups rapidly came together in the Central Citizens' Defence Committee (CCDC), which, just as rapidly, was taken over by men who were determined to resurrect a rearmed IRA as the dominant force of nationalist Belfast.

Fifteen-year-old Bradley never went back to school again. In those days fifteen was the school-leaving age. He did not start work either. Following the traumatic events of August 1969, he and his friends were organised as lookouts. 'We took turns to watch day and night for attacks from the Shankill. We were messengers, carrying information between the men of the district who were manning barricades and acting as vigilantes. From the top floors of the flats we could watch the derelict houses beyond the waste ground and see well into the lower Shankill. We removed the lights along the balconies in Unity Flats and we broke any that were replaced so that movements in the flats could not be seen from the Shankill.'

For the first fortnight after the disturbances on 2 August, they stood ready to repel police coming near Unity Flats, partly because of what they had seen the police do in the August riots, but also because the police were seeking retribution against the teenage stone-throwers. Paddy Kennedy, the area's Stormont MP, complained about this police activity. He said they were arresting innocent boys of fifteen and sixteen, bringing them to the barracks and charging them with throwing stones in Unity Walk. 'They do not know they were even there. They have no evidence against them. I have evidence the police are coming in and saying, "OK. I will take this one." They have never even seen them before but they go to court, swear away their lives on oath and secure convictions against the innocent people of Carrick Hill, Unity Place and Unity Walk, who are only out to defend their property.'

After the arrival of the British army, it became impossible for the RUC to get into Unity, or, indeed, any other nationalist district in Belfast. Soldiers stood on guard at the entrances to prevent loyalist incursions, and the police stayed away. The older men of the district acted as vigilantes, standing by barricades all with hurley sticks, hammers and other makeshift weapons at the ready. In October 1969, the district's Westminster MP Gerry Fitt, who was also a Stormont MP, described the conditions to the Stormont parliament:

> I represent a small constituency in Dock where men are roaming the streets night after night to prevent an incursion from another area … and when men, if they are at work, are giving up hours when they should be in their beds asleep in order to protect their homes and the safety of their women and children.

October 1969 was another bad month for Unity Flats. On 10 October, to the consternation of hard-line unionists, a report by Lord Hunt, whom the British government had asked to inquire into policing, recommended the disarming of the RUC and the disbandment of the B Specials, an ill-trained, notoriously anti-Catholic armed police reserve. Two nights after the publication of Hunt's report, a huge mob marched down the Shankill, its sights once again set on Unity Flats as the most convenient symbol of nationalist aspiration. UVF men in the crowd opened fire on an RUC cordon across the Shankill Road, killing the first police victim of the troubles, Constable Victor Arbuckle (by coincidence, in August, Constable Arbuckle had driven the Land Rover that took the fatally injured Patrick Corry from Unity Flats to hospital after he had been batoned by police). Following the shooting of Arbuckle, British soldiers then took over and dispersed the Unionist crowd, shooting two men dead.

Unity Flats continued to be a target for the anger of people from the Shankill. Their MP, Johnny McQuade, whipped up the flames of antagonism. When repeated assaults failed, McQuade, in a speech on the Shankill in January 1970, called for the whole complex to be cleared and converted into offices. Desmond Boal QC, MP for Shankill and close to Rev. Ian Paisley, who was present at the meeting, hotly denied he made any similar remarks, though the *Belfast Newsletter* carried the headlines, 'Clear Unity Flats asks Woodvale MP' and 'Angry Crowds Block Shankill'.

Paddy Kennedy MP took both Boal and McQuade to task at Stormont on 28 January. He said Unity Flats had been attacked five times since August by

> hostile and undisciplined mobs, sometimes armed, coming down the Shankill Road. Many residents [of Unity] have had all their windows smashed by stones and bricks. Some windows are blocked up for up to three months because of attacks and residents have to use increased electricity in daylight. Women and children have to stay up all night.

A month earlier, in December 1969, according to Gerry Bradley, guns had arrived in Unity Flats and were hidden away for defence against any future incursion. 'I didn't know where they came from. I assumed Dublin. That's what everybody thought. Men from republican families took control of the guns. A "republican family" was one where the men had been in the IRA in the 1940s, maybe interned in the 1950s during what they called the "border campaign" .'

To his surprise, Bradley discovered that his was a republican family of impeccable pedigree. 'My father, Willie Bradley, had been in the IRA and had been sent to England on a bombing mission in 1939 when the IRA "declared war" on Britain. A bomb he was to plant partially exploded prematurely, injuring his arm. He escaped the police hunt after the explosion, but as he was waiting on the platform for a train to Holyhead, a porter spotted blood dripping from his arm, and he was arrested. He was sentenced to ten years in jail, most of which he served in Dartmoor, where he was "on the blanket", claiming to be a prisoner of war and refusing to wear prison clothes or do prison work. He also went on a dirty protest, refusing to slop out. As a result, he got no remission and served nine years, nine months and twenty-eight days. My mother also came from a republican family. She had married my father, Willie Bradley, not long before he went to England in 1939. Since he refused to cooperate with the prison regime for most of his sentence, she saw him only four times in the ten years he spent in jail.'

After Willie Bradley and others in England were arrested, the unionist government at Stormont introduced internment without trial. His three brothers, Anthony, John and Jamesy, also known republicans, were swept up. Interning republicans was the normal response of the Stormont administration to any IRA activity. Two of Mrs Bradley's brothers, Gerry and Tommy McCotter, were also interned, while a third, Sammy, was sentenced to six months as a member of a Fianna (junior IRA) group arrested after being found training on the Cave Hill, the mountain outcrop that dominates north Belfast. Some years later, John

Bradley, Willie's brother, was one of the last men in the North sentenced to be flogged with the cat o'nine tails. He lost a kidney in jail after savage beatings by warders.

'I didn't know any of this before August 1969. My father had died in 1966 in Turf Lodge, where we had been housed temporarily while Unity Flats were being built. He had a republican funeral, complete with tricolour-draped coffin. He had refused the last rites of the Catholic Church because he had been excommunicated in the 1940s for supporting the IRA's campaign and he never had any time for the Church after that. I was twelve when he died and I didn't know any of this family history and I didn't understand what all the stuff about the funeral, the flag and all, was about. In the forty-eight hours after the riots of 2–4 August, I heard more about the IRA than I had in my whole life to that point. Before those events no one had spoken of the family's history.'

His ignorance about his family's republican past would have been the norm in republican families. In the 1960s in Belfast, the IRA and republicans in general were discredited and shunned. By the mid-1960s, for practical purposes, the IRA had ceased to exist. People looked down on former members or republican activists and were afraid to be seen associating with them in case their own prospects were damaged or they attracted the attention of the RUC Special Branch. If a former IRA man had a job, the police would be sure to inform his employer of his dubious background and he was likely to be given his cards. Employers did not want police around their business. 'So it was difficult for republicans to get a job. Former internees and convicted men found it impossible. Only Eastwoods scrap merchants in Andersonstown [then on the outskirts of west Belfast] employed them as labourers, and then at very low wages.'

After the ignominious failure of the border campaign – six years of attacks on customs posts and RUC barracks near the border, which ended in 1962 – the IRA leadership in Dublin was changing direction in the mid-sixties towards becoming a Marxist-inspired political movement. In any case, the border campaign had had no effect on the remnants of the IRA in Belfast, though the unionist government had interned several as a precaution. In this atmosphere of defeat and depression, Bradley's mother had not tried to inculcate any republicanism in him or his brother. It seemed there was no future in it. It was over. As events turned out, the opposite was the case.

After the attacks on Unity Flats, Gerry Bradley would view in a new light the people he was familiar with as friends of his parents, who had visited their Carrick Hill home regularly: men like Billy McKee, Jimmy Steele, John Kelly and Frankie Card (later known as Proinsias MacAirt) from Clonard in west Belfast. These men, life-long republicans, who disagreed with the political, Marxist direction republican leaders in Dublin had been taking, were soon to be among the leading figures in the new IRA in Belfast. They and others in Unity Flats told Bradley about his family, and his mother and father's backgrounds.

Suddenly, other people who had been introverted and secretive and of no significance in society were speaking openly, recalling past IRA actions, as long ago as the 1920s when Carrick Hill had also been under constant attack from the Shankill and the newly constituted RUC and B Specials. Bradley learnt that his grandmother McCotter was well known for throwing holy water at police in cage cars when they came to raid her house in Upton Street in Carrick Hill!

From being ignored and ostracised, republicans, after August 1969, instantly became important figures in the district. They appeared justified, vindicated. People in the 1960s who had said the days of the troubles, as the period 1920-22 was then called, were over, had been proved wrong. Republicans, who had been derided for prophesying that it would all happen again, had been proved right. People looked to them now as the only available defenders of their community from possible destruction. And people expected them to produce guns. It was a development common to all the districts in Belfast that suffered in 1969. Even in districts that hadn't, like the huge Andersonstown estate, there was also widespread, though less open, support for a resurgent IRA. After all, what alternative was there when people had just witnessed the behaviour of the police in Belfast and Derry? It was clear from recent events that, far from protecting nationalist communities, the police had either stood by and watched people's homes burning or facilitated the onslaughts. Hundreds of young men in such districts clamoured to join the IRA.

One of them was Gerry Bradley. 'I was too young. Seventeen

was the minimum age for joining the IRA. Me and my mates had to join the Fianna [Fianna na hÉireann, a sort of junior, or youth wing of the IRA]. I reckon that by 1971 there were at least fifty members of the Fianna and Cumann na gCailíní, [the girls' equivalent] in Unity Flats alone, half of the boys and girls my age in the district. At the time I joined, in 1970, there was no IRA campaign. It was all defence.'

The members of the Provisional IRA, which had just been established in opposition to the Marxist Dublin leadership, saw its role in Belfast as trying to reassure people that the events of summer 1969 would never happen again because there would be guns available. The re-emergence of the IRA was a reaction to the RUC's actions and growing loyalist violence. The next time there was a loyalist attack, the IRA would be ready.

In June 1970, the reconstituted IRA had its first opportunity to play the role it had taken upon itself. It turned out to be a pivotal point in the emergence of the new IRA in Belfast. Rioting began in north Belfast on the Crumlin Road at Ardoyne after an Orange march in west Belfast provoked confrontations in several parts of Belfast. In an exchange of up to two hundred shots across the Crumlin Road, Martin Meehan's IRA company in Ardoyne shot and killed three men on the loyalist side of the Crumlin Road. Later that night, the IRA repulsed a loyalist attack on St Matthew's Catholic church in the Short Strand. Here is the account of the incident by Colonel Michael Dewar in his book *The British Army in Northern Ireland*.

In the Short Strand area the PIRA Belfast Brigade commander Billy McKee, and his 3rd battalion commander, Billy Kelly, supported by local volunteers, defended St Matthew's church against Protestant gunmen. The shooting went on until 5am by which time two Protestants had been killed; another two died later from their injuries and several more were wounded. One PIRA man was killed and McKee was wounded. The whole incident had taken its course because the army was so chronically overstretched that night in Belfast. The one spare platoon in the whole of West Belfast was not able to get through rioting Protestants to the Short Strand.

These incidents in Ardoyne and the Short Strand secured the Belfast IRA's reputation as defenders of the nationalist community, a consequence Colonel Dewar openly accepted. In both cases, the British army did too little too late, with disastrous consequences for its credibility among nationalists.

Bradley says: 'The St Matthew's incident made the Provos. It showed they could do the biz. After that, every year until 2003 every [IRA] company in third batt was on standby from 11–14 July. There was a drink ban on volunteers in Ardoyne, Unity and the Short Strand. Each area had a group of volunteers on standby at any given time. They stayed in standby houses, four or five volunteers in each house. The "gear" [firearms] would be a couple of streets away. It wasn't just over the Twelfth. Any time there was a loyalist parade, there were volunteers on standby in whatever third batt company area the parade was going through. Guys could be transferred from other areas where needed.'

Thanks to the admitted failure of the British army in June 1970, the IRA had shown its mettle as the protector of the nationalist community in Belfast. Acquiring weapons to defend Catholic streets against attack had been the original impetus for breaking with the Dublin leadership in late 1969, but the men who formed the Provisional IRA in Belfast had bigger fish to fry. Ostensibly, the British army had been deployed to defend the nationalist community from loyalist onslaughts, but, as far as republicans were concerned, the real purpose of the army was to defend the Unionist administration at Stormont, which was under intense pressure from Westminster to bring in radical reforms that would satisfy the nationalist community. Those republicans who formed the Provisional IRA believed Stormont could not and should not be reformed. They aimed to end partition and believed that if they could make the North ungovernable and bring about the collapse of Stormont, then they could negotiate a British withdrawal and end partition.

Therefore, while the emphasis in 1970 was on defence, the Provisionals strove to ensure that there would be no return to the status quo before 1969 – that no amount of reforms would pacify the North. They intended to render the North unworkable. As Charles Haughey used to repeat well into the 1980s, 'The North is a failed political entity.' The Provisionals agreed. They were not about to participate in making it a success. Their attitude was summed up in the phrase, 'To hell with your reforms, give us back our country.' The firm belief of thousands like Gerry Bradley was that, in view of what they had seen and experienced in 1969, there was no chance of achieving equality in the North unless partition was ended. For that to happen, the British army had to be driven out. Only then would Unionists agree to negotiate on equal terms.

Already by spring 1970, the new IRA leadership began to lay the foundations for a major offensive. For the first time ever in the North, they had the manpower, but they needed weapons. It would not be long before they arrived. 'Guys like Billy McKee [the IRA leader in Belfast] realised they had something they could use. They had masses of recruits. You could wait six months then before getting into the 'RA.' In Dublin, Seán MacStíofáin, Ruairí Ó Brádaigh and Daithi Ó Conaill saw they could build an army, a prospect they had dreamed of since the 1940s. Throughout 1970 the new IRA was growing into that army.

Without weapons in any numbers, the first stage of the offensive was organised daily rioting in parts of Belfast and Derry, with the British army as the target. Inevitably, the rioting provoked stronger and stronger responses from the army, initially baton charges, then the infamous CS tear gas, fired in ever-increasing quantities, then rubber bullets. In these riots, members of the Fianna played a front-line role. Bradley participated in riots that took place every Friday and Saturday night in Castle Street, where the Falls district meets Belfast city centre. It was almost a sport.

'I went there about 9.00 or 10.00pm and waited until there was a big enough crowd of boys from places like Ardoyne, Divis or Clonard, all districts of west and north Belfast where loyalist gangs had burned people out of their homes in 1969, with and without police help. We'd stand around outside dancehalls called the Astor and Romanos, but we'd no intention of going into either of these establishments to enjoy the showbands. When the crowd had gathered, we began stoning the nearby police barracks in Queen Street, hoping to lure the police out for a street battle. We had girlfriends there and they wanted to go to Romanos to dance – I remember going in once. But I didn't go down there to dance. I went to riot. I had no teenage life.'

Bradley remembers crowds of up to five hundred rioting near the city centre each weekend; this figure is confirmed by newspaper reports from the time. But his activities were not confined to the city centre.

The IRA took care about the location of riots. In the sprawling Ballymurphy estate in west Belfast, with its population of thousands, rioting was endemic, with the army firing CS gas into crowds on a daily basis. In certain weather the smell of gas hung over the streets all day. On the other hand, 'the IRA did not allow Unity Flats to riot or open fire in 1970 because it was too small and could not be defended if the army decided to take on the rioters. We weren't allowed to riot in Unity. The 'RA threatened us. They were sometimes moving gear and we'd be bringing the army in by starting a riot. We didn't know and they didn't tell us. Anyway, it needled us that we weren't allowed to riot. I loved rioting. So did my mates. We used to travel to Ardoyne or Ballymurphy instead. Six, eight or ten of us would get taxis to the "Murph". The Murph was the best. There'd be hundreds and hundreds rioting. It was the real thing: CS gas, British army "snatch squads". If they caught you, you were in for a pasting.'

The police were the enemy because of what they had done in 1969. These riots were a chance to fight the police, to get back at them, but soon it was the British army facing the rioters as a matter of course. Bradley, like most of his Fianna colleagues, was eventually arrested and convicted of riotous behaviour in 1970. He received a six-month suspended sentence.

If the riots were a pretext for Fianna members and nationalist teenagers generally to 'get back at the police', they also had other purposes for the IRA leaders who encouraged them. They helped to destabilise Belfast. They kept the army on the streets in aggressive mode. They helped to 'blood' members of the Fianna. They helped to isolate the security forces from the nationalist community and provoke them into ever more aggressive tactics to quell the rioting. Continual rioting helped to radicalise and politicise the community. Soon, however, the rioting began to take a back seat. It had served its purpose.

The newly formed Provisional IRA was bringing in guns to Belfast as quickly as they could, and also began to detonate bombs in Belfast in 1970. One of the first bombs, in March 1970, destroyed a statue of a nineteenth-century Protestant hero, 'Roaring' Hanna, a firebrand preacher who reminded many people of Ian Paisley. Gerry O'Neill, an IRA man from Unity Flats, blew the statue off its plinth in the centre of Carlisle Circus, leaving only a pair of bronze boots behind. Carlisle Circus is a hallowed spot for Unionists where the annual Belfast Orange parade begins each twelfth of July, but, conveniently for the IRA, it was also just a hundred metres from Unity Flats.

The IRA was also beginning to take control of the nationalist districts barricaded off since August 1969, districts known to the security forces as 'NOGO areas'. There were no police or British army in these districts, so gradually the IRA took upon themselves the role of policing. IRA members went openly on patrol, sometimes carrying weapons. They disciplined troublesome youths by giving them a hiding, or, in cases of what came to be called 'anti-social behaviour', they broke bones or tarred and feathered youths, and occasionally girls who fraternised with British soldiers. Serious misdemeanours were dealt with by shooting the culprit in the leg, a practice later 'refined' as 'knee-capping'.

An IRA command structure was established. In the Belfast Brigade, which Billy McKee ran at the outset of the campaign, there were three battalions, each with several companies. The first and second battalions, literally the big battalions, covered west Belfast. Unity Flats fell into the third battalion's area, which covered north Belfast's nationalist districts: Ardoyne, the Bone, Newington, the New Lodge and Legoniel, but also isolated districts like the Bawnmore estate near loyalist Rathcoole in north Belfast, the Markets near the centre of Belfast and the Short Strand in east Belfast. According to Bradley, 'all these areas were under constant attack from loyalists.' Unlike west Belfast, a huge homogeneous nationalist area, beginning to stretch towards Lisburn, each of the districts in the third battalion area was a Catholic enclave, either facing onto or completely surrounded by a loyalist area. IRA men had to travel from the larger districts in the third battalion area, like Ardoyne and the New Lodge, to defend the smaller districts like the Markets, and especially the beleaguered Short Strand on the 'wrong' side of the River Lagan where about 3,000 nationalists were hemmed in against the Lagan by 60,000 Unionists.

Unity Flats IRA originally formed C company of the third battalion, but as the IRA grew rapidly, particularly after internment in 1971, the number of companies had to be increased from three to seven to accommodate the influx of volunteers. By early 1972, Unity Flats was to become the home base of G company of the third battalion of the IRA's Belfast Brigade. Bradley estimates that by 1972 there were about thirty trained IRA members, men and women, in G company, supported by about fifty auxiliaries and forty to fifty Fianna (boys) and Cailíní (girls), aged fourteen to sixteen. Auxiliaries tended to be in their thirties, too old for 'operations', which, in the early seventies in Belfast, usually involved shooting, then running with your heart pounding.

Rioting and throwing petrol bombs at the British army fulfilled several functions, but for much of 1970 there was little else the IRA could do. They did not have enough weapons to mount any kind of onslaught, nor did they have either enough explosives or the personnel with the expertise to make bombs. But the IRA set about remedying these deficiencies. In Belfast in early 1971, they selected groups of four men from each of the three battalions and sent them to camps in the Republic for weapons training. 'I was one of the ones selected from the third battalion. I was selected like the others, as able and willing lads. I learned on pistols and .22 and .303 rifles. I liked the target practice and using live rounds. They had set up makeshift firing ranges in barns and cowsheds. I was quite good at it.'

Crawling about in open country at night, though, was another matter. Bradley was fit enough to do it all right, but to him it was 'just silly' for guys from Belfast. They were all covered in mud and usually soaking wet. What was the point? When would they ever use anything they learned in the open countryside? On the other hand, what was the alternative? The IRA could not train in the North with the British army constantly patrolling the countryside, and they certainly could not build mock-ups of Belfast streets as the British army did in England to train their squaddies. Bradley trained mainly to be a gunman. Other teenagers and men in their twenties were sent to camps for explosives officers where they were trained in the mysteries of bomb-making and electrical circuitry. On their return to Belfast, some of them were expected to train others in weaponry and bomb-making techniques, and so the expertise spread.

Once he had weapons training and some knowledge of explosives, like others in the Belfast IRA, what Bradley relied on was his intimate knowledge of his own locality, which over the years extended beyond Unity Flats to Ardoyne, the rest of north Belfast, the Markets and Short Strand. As for south Belfast and east Belfast beyond the Short Strand, he 'hadn't a clue'. Everywhere else outside Belfast was 'the country', *terra incognita.*

'I don't remember women going to camps in the Republic, but if it hadn't been for the women of the district, the IRA would have been out of business early on and the support of the women always remained an essential requirement.' Years later, Gerry Adams said, 'The day the women throw the guns out in the street the IRA is finished.' However, it was not only that many women helped to hide weapons and explosives and men and to move materiel. That is taken for granted. What is not generally appreciated is the number of women who were active IRA members, regularly participating in operations. Bradley says, 'The women were brilliant. The army could not have succeeded without the women.'

Before the emergence of the Provisional IRA in 1970, the women's version of the IRA was a separate organisation called Cumann na mBan, literally 'the women's club'. Traditionally, Cumann na mBan members were very much auxiliaries, literally helping out. After the Provisional IRA emerged, attempts by older women, the existing members in Cumann na mBan, to enforce the old rules were scorned by the influx of new female recruits who wanted to use guns and explosives. After all, it was the early seventies, the era of Women's Lib. The new members were not going to be satisfied with making tea and sandwiches or rolling bandages during a riot. Very quickly, Cumann na mBan vanished and became subsumed within the IRA.

'Women became full members of companies. They went to gun

lectures with the men. They were treated the same. They did ops [operations]: bank robberies, shooting, bombing. They got taken to Castlereagh too. They got terrible verbal and physical abuse from the RUC there. It was actually worse for them than the men, because the cops took it out on them because they were women. It wasn't just girls. A lot of them were married women with kids. Some of them were middle-aged. The senior IRA woman in the New Lodge, Minnie Loughran, had her son shot dead by the Brits, and he was in his thirties. Other women who never joined the 'RA and stayed civilians, did as much as IRA members. One woman in Unity, Annie McCann – her home was open house for IRA operators. She would have hidden anything or anybody. She had her eightieth birthday in 2007.'

Of course, one of the forces driving women into the IRA was the assault on Catholic districts in 1969. According to the Scarman Report, about 1,800 families had been displaced in August 1969, of whom 1,500 were Catholics. Scarman estimated that 5.3 percent of Catholic households in Belfast were compelled to move, but that percentage was concentrated in three or four districts where whole streets of houses were burnt. People lost everything. Many ended up in friends' houses or squatting illegally in empty or semi-derelict houses. Many women who joined the IRA did so because they were determined such events would never happen again. Some joined because they were personally affected, having lost their homes; others because friends or relatives had suffered. They were resolved to defend their districts from marauding loyalists and the police, whom many of the women had witnessed aiding and abetting the loyalist mobs.

Many held traditional, strong republican convictions that seemed vindicated by the events of 1969. They simply believed that the only hope for fairness and justice was Irish unity, that the major obstacle to that was the British government presence in Ireland and that the way to remove that obstacle was to drive the British army out.

The other powerful force propelling women into the IRA was the misbehaviour of the British army, beginning in summer 1970 and rising to a crescendo during internment in August 1971 and in the months immediately following. Husbands, fathers, sons and brothers were gratuitously assaulted by soldiers in the street. Some were badly beaten and never fully recovered. Soldiers attacked local youths, beat them off the streets, picked fights during searches of local pubs and generally humiliated the population. The women, disgusted by the soldiers' treatment of their menfolk, were delighted when the IRA hit back. Some resolved to hit back themselves.

Assaults were only one aspect of British military misbehaviour. What drove women to despair was the destruction of the furnishings and fabric of their homes by troops as they carried out raids and searches. No one was ever allowed to film a British army search in the North of Ireland, as they kicked in doors, ripped up floorboards, broke down stud walls, tore down ceilings. Districts like Unity Flats and the New Lodge were repeatedly sealed off and searched, sometimes on a house-to-house basis. As the army admitted themselves, they did not have enough intelligence in the early days to enable them to pinpoint a particular house where weapons or explosives were concealed. Raids were mostly speculative. It did not seem to matter that the families affected would be enemies forever.

Between November 1971 and March 1972, Stormont Hansard records that there were 10,366 properties searched in Northern Ireland, 8,505 of them in Belfast. Arms and ammunition were found in a grand total of 87 premises. After Operation Motorman in the summer of 1972, when the army occupied Catholic districts, the number of searches increased exponentially. In 1974 there were 74,914 house searches, usually in the same districts, and often the same houses and streets repeatedly.

For the Belfast IRA, while Unity Flats was small and vulnerable to attack, one of its main advantages was its location, five minutes' walk to the centre of Belfast. The IRA's first bombs in Belfast city centre exploded in 1970. One of the first places to suffer was North Street, the main route into the city centre from the Shankill Road, but also the main route from Unity Flats. There was a Woolworth's in North Street and a number of wallpaper and paint shops, pubs, butchers and electrical shops. Bradley says, quite simply, 'We destroyed North Street.' It has never recovered.

Bombs were carried into the city centre in biscuit tins and cardboard boxes. Others were carried in shopping bags. Bigger ones came on the short journey from Unity Flats by car. Over the years, women members of Unity Flats' G company also fire-bombed dozens of shops in the city centre, and then walked home, anonymous among hundreds of other women shoppers. Bradley reels off a list of names of IRA women, some of whom cannot return to the North of Ireland and others who have died of natural causes, like Cindy Horn and Lily Valente.

'Cindy Horn blew up umpteen places in Belfast and burned loads down with incendiaries. It was up to the women to decide where to plant incendiaries. They looked for sprinkler systems. They knew the type of clothing that would burn and set the whole place on fire. In the end it didn't matter where they planted them, as long as they got rid of the incendiaries, but they always tried to do the best job. The majority of those bombs were planted by two-women teams. Sometimes one woman went alone. They usually went well-dressed, like office workers. They knew how to get past checks. Women were also brilliant at intelligence work, pretending to walk kids, push prams, get into places, nose around.' It was no wonder that for one British officer writing in the seventies, G company was 'the most dangerous [IRA unit] in Ulster'.

3

MAYHEM

'When I was first handed a gun, I felt: this is it, the real thing.
I was excited. I felt fear. I was apprehensive. I felt responsible.
They gave you a gun for a purpose and it was to defend the people in
Unity. That's what I was for. It meant I had moved beyond
the street rioting. I had power, some control.
I wasn't on my own, of course.
I was part of a company. Now, instead of me rioting,
I was one of the ones using the rioting.'

The IRA strategy to isolate the British army and brand them as enemies was successful by the summer of 1970. By that stage, all the efforts of the British army to build relationships with the Catholic population had failed. Since arriving on the streets in August 1969, the army had tried football matches with senior pupils in local schools, they had played water-polo matches in the Falls swimming baths with local teams, they had organised swimming galas and discos, but by early summer 1970 no one was taking up army invitations.

'I never took part in any of their football matches. I don't know anybody in Unity who did. We knew what it was about from the start. It was so obvious. I would certainly have discouraged anybody from getting involved. The army organised matches and things with St Malachy's College [about 400 metres from Unity, one of the two Catholic boys' grammar schools in Belfast then], but that had nothing to do with us. We kept them at arm's length from the start.'

The relationship between the army and the Catholic population had broken down in clouds of CS gas, house searches and beatings. The definitive breach was caused by what was known as the 'Falls Road curfew' in July 1970, when, following a large find of arms and explosives, the army sealed off the whole lower Falls district for two days and carried out house-to-house searches. During the period of the curfew, three people died from gunfire and one was crushed by an army vehicle. Sixty-eight civilians were injured and about twenty soldiers were wounded in gun battles. Army figures show troops fired 1,427 live rounds in the densely built-up district from their high-velocity NATO-issue SLR assault rifles. The deaths and injuries to the civilian population were compounded by individual soldiers damaging property and personal possessions in houses, and others, notably members of the Black Watch regiment, stealing cash, watches and jewellery.

Parallel to the rioting and organised street disturbances in 1970, the number of IRA shooting incidents and explosions increased as weapons arrived and expertise with explosives developed. In

August, the IRA in south Armagh killed two RUC men in an explosion, the first police casualties of the IRA campaign. In February 1971, the IRA in north Belfast shot and killed the first British soldier to die. The size and frequency of disturbances increased and the weight of explosives detonated grew. By the beginning of 1971, it was clear the IRA had access to large numbers of guns and explosives and scores of members trained for gun battles. A full-scale campaign was under way.

The unionist prime minister, Major James Chichester-Clark, resigned in March 1971 when the British government refused to send extra troops. His successor, Brian Faulkner, from the outset was privately demanding internment without trial, which, as Stormont Minister of Home Affairs, he had implemented during the IRA border campaign in the 1950s. The British government was very reluctant to accede to his demands, especially since the advice of the army top brass was that internment would not solve the underlying problems in the North and could make matters worse. However, on the night before the twelfth of July Orange parade in 1971, the Belfast IRA mounted a bomb blitz along Royal Avenue, the city-centre route of the parade, which left Orangemen picking their way through rubble between bombed-out shop fronts as venetian blinds and curtains flapped through smashed window frames. It was the last straw. The British government agreed to internment. On 9 August, British army units arrested 342 people in nationalist districts across the North.

Internment produced a tidal wave of opposition among

nationalists. There was, of course, the fundamental objection in principle to internment without trial, an objection strenuously articulated not only by nationalists, but by members of the British Labour party and the Irish government. Then, the implementation of internment was made so much more obnoxious by the fact that only Catholics had been interned. By spring 1972 the number of internees was approaching a thousand.

The IRA company in Unity Flats had played an important role in planting the bombs in Royal Avenue on the night of 11 July, which had clinched the decision to implement internment: Royal Avenue was only 200 metres from Unity Flats. Ironically, no one in Unity Flats, IRA or otherwise, was arrested – or 'lifted' as people termed it – on the day of internment a month later in August 1971. The internment operation drew a blank in Unity Flats, but caused intense resentment and hostility in other areas.

Several reasons explain this failure by the security forces. First, as the frequency of shooting and bombing increased markedly through 1971, most IRA men had been expecting internment, as that had always been the response of Unionist governments. Many of them had already gone on the run before the first sweep began on 9 August. Besides, the intelligence the RUC gave the British army, who carried out the internment operation, was lamentably wrong and out of date. All the senior IRA figures in Belfast escaped the first sweep – and the IRA leaders held a press conference the next day in St Thomas's secondary school in west Belfast to prove it.

However, the introduction of internment had an unlooked-for

effect. It provided a major boost for the IRA careers of people like Gerry Bradley. With the senior men on the run, young and irresponsible figures like Bradley really came into their own across the city. By the summer of 1971, Bradley was a fully-trained IRA member and chafing at the bit to get into action, but the men in command in Unity Flats kept youths like him on a tight rein. Just as well: there was no telling what they might get up to.

For example, in 1970 Bradley and a friend, Micky Kelly, off their own bat, had tried to set fire to Clifton Street Orange hall, a hundred metres from Unity. It was no ordinary Orange hall, but the most important in Belfast. Located in Carlisle Circus beside the biggest Presbyterian church in the world, the hall was, and remains to this day, the point of departure for the annual twelfth of July parade in Belfast, which forms up in Carlisle Circus. Bearing the marks of scores of attacks, the hall's classical pediment is adorned with the only equestrian statue in Belfast, a bronze King William of Orange. Flanking the statue are flagpoles that fly a Union Jack and an 'Ulster' flag (a loyalist confection of a white flag with the red cross of St George, and, in the middle, a red hand of Ulster with a British crown on it) throughout every July and August. Protective wire caging was removed from the hall façade – only in March 2009 – after a £30,000 makeover.

Bradley and Kelly managed to break open the back doors of the hall. They had acquired tea chests, which they filled with inflammable material, lit it, then triumphantly carried the blazing tea chests aloft on their heads into the hall and deposited them where they reckoned the blaze would catch best. As they ran out of the back doors, they were caught by a patrol of the King's Own Scottish Borderers and hauled off to the soldiers' base on the lower Shankill Road. Luckily for Bradley, one of the respected community leaders in Unity Flats, Emmanuel O'Rourke (he who had taken on four policemen in August 1969), went to the army base and was able to convince the officer in charge that, rather than setting fire to the place, Bradley and Kelly had been there because O'Rourke had ordered them into the hall to try to extinguish the fire, and that the pair of them had run out when the flames got out of control. Bradley says O'Rourke gave them 'a slap' for the escapade.

The escapade in itself is of no significance other than to illustrate the type of madness the teenagers in the IRA were capable of. It never occurred to Bradley what the repercussions would have been for Unity Flats if he had succeeded in burning down the most iconic Orange hall in the North. It would not simply have been a matter of risk for Unity Flats and its inhabitants, but there would, in all likelihood, have been retaliation against nearby Catholic churches, especially St Patrick's cathedral, the parish church of the residents of Unity.

Even so, Bradley is unrepentant. 'I was just looking at Clifton Street Orange hall recently and thinking if me and Kelly had managed to burn it down it wouldn't be there today.'

The unforeseen consequence of internment was that youths like Bradley were unleashed on Belfast. Initially they had no 'gear', as he calls it. 'Gear' meant primarily guns, but also explosives. The gear was controlled by the local IRA OC, or 'officer commanding', and his quartermaster. It was carefully hidden in dumps.

In the absence of 'gear', the location of which only a couple of IRA men in the district knew, the teenage IRA members and Fianna in Unity Flats simply rioted in response to the appearance of British army arrest squads intent on interning men. In practice, this meant that dozens of local youths poured out of Unity Flats, hijacked cars, vans, lorries and buses, set fire to them and blocked the main roads out of Belfast city centre and past Unity Flats with the burning vehicles. They threw stones, bricks, bottles and petrol bombs at any members of police or army who came within range. According to Bradley, the days after 9 August 1971 were 'mayhem'. The statistics bear him out.

If C company, as it then was in Unity, could not get to weapons, A company in Ardoyne certainly did, and fierce gun battles raged night and day in which IRA members, British soldiers and civilians, men and women, were killed. The same was true on an even larger scale in west Belfast. Palls of black smoke hung over nationalist districts of Belfast for days as buildings and vehicles burnt. The thump of explosions reverberated in the city centre and around the big nationalist districts, and gunfire rattled day and night. Eleven people were shot dead in Belfast on 9 August alone, and in the following week another nine were killed. Dozens were injured by gunfire, explosions and missiles of various kinds, thrown by opposing factions. An official report by the

Northern Ireland Housing Executive indicated that at least 2,500 families moved house in the three weeks after internment began, most in fierce sectarian clashes in north Belfast, where two streets of houses were burnt in Ardoyne.

Many in the British government were furious with the unionist ministers at Stormont, who had convinced them that internment would bring an end to the escalating violence. Instead, the opposite was the result. Paradoxically, one of the most forthright condemnations of the whole exercise was given by the clever, lazy, financially corrupt British politician Reginald Maudling, who was Home Secretary at the time. Unfortunately, his condemnation came twenty years after the event. In an interview with the *Independent* newspaper in 1991, Maudling, speaking with the advantage of hindsight said

> The experience of internment, from 1971 to 1975, was by almost universal consent an unmitigated disaster, which has left an indelible mark on the history of Northern Ireland. It did not conform to international human rights standards because many of the wrong people were picked up and because it was accompanied by casual brutality during and after the arrests. It was also seen as an illegitimate weapon, in that part of the reason for using it was to prop up an ailing Unionist government.

For more than a year, no loyalists were rounded up, while republicans were kept in miserable conditions in leaky Nissen huts. On the outside, the death toll rose alarmingly, while riots and street disturbances became much worse. Thousands of people moved home.

Alienation rose sharply in the Catholic population, thousands becoming involved in rent-and-rates strikes and civil disobedience.

For Gerry Bradley the imposition of internment began one of the most frenzied periods of his life. Eventually, of course, he and his pals did get their hands on the gear. The senior men who had escaped the internment sweep were soon back in their districts, districts which, it should be remembered, were still barricaded 'NOGO areas', as they had been since August 1969. With guns and explosives available, the IRA's dozens of trained operatives were ready to repulse any onslaught by British army arrest teams. The IRA also had the support of most people in the communities where they lived. The obvious burning injustice of internment, with so many innocents arrested and beaten, produced a furious response and a solidarity among the people whose husbands, fathers, brothers and sons had been maltreated and slung into Maudling's miserable, leaky huts.

Bradley says: 'In 1971 it wasn't republicans in the third battalion: it was the people. The areas of the third batt were constantly under attack from loyalists, from British army raids. The IRA were the defenders of the area. You had a hundred houses to stay in. Every door was open. Popular support was enormous. Everybody was behind us. We genuinely believed we could beat the Brits this time.'

For a couple of months after August 1971, as a result of internment, the British army was facing an uprising in Catholic districts of Belfast and Derry. This much is admitted in the army's official 'Analysis of Military Operations in Northern Ireland', prepared for the Chief of the General Staff, Sir Mike Jackson, in 2006. The document describes the period from August 1971 to the mid-seventies as 'a classic insurgency'. My own research reveals that between August 1969 and August 1971, fewer than 100 people had been killed. In the months between August 1971 and December 1971, about 150 were killed. Between August 1969 and August 1971, nine British soldiers were killed. Between August 1971 and the end of the year, thirty-three were killed. It was not only gun battles that the security forces had to contend with. Scores of explosions began to reduce Belfast's commercial centre to rubble. Mayhem indeed.

Young men like Bradley firmly believed they had right on their side. 'We saw ourselves defending people against an occupying army which was coming into our district every day, wrecking all round them, and their reason for being in the North at all was to shore up an unjust regime, just as the British army had always done in Ireland.'

In the first sweep, in August, 342 men had been 'lifted' across the North, but so cock-eyed had the RUC intelligence been that 104 were released within 48 hours. The horror stories those released men told about their brutal treatment by the British army fuelled the resistance that people like Bradley were engaged in, and explained the unquestioning support of people in the Catholic districts affected. Internment finally ended any legitimacy the Stormont government ever had among the Catholic population.

By August 1971, Bradley had graduated to using guns. 'I

couldn't wait to get using a gun. I'd been doing training and all that. I knew how to use it, but it wasn't the same. When I was first handed a gun, I felt: this is it, the real thing. I was excited. I felt fear. I was apprehensive. I felt responsible. They gave you a gun for a purpose and it was to defend the people in Unity. That's what I was for. It meant I had moved beyond the street rioting. I had power, some control. I wasn't on my own, of course. I was part of a company. Now, instead of me rioting, I was one of the ones using the rioting.

'While the kids were rioting, we got gear and moved it, used them as cover. We'd say, "Start a riot and get the Brits round to such and such a place." The kids knew what was going on. I know because I'd been one of them not so long before. The kids knew the plan. The Brits would come on to confront the stone-throwers and we'd open up, fire forty or fifty shots, scatter them, maybe hit one.'

Bradley believed, 'We couldn't be bate. We were winning gun battles against the Brits. They had everything: armoured cars, the law, firepower, manpower, CS gas, and still they couldn't win. I genuinely believed that one day the IRA would be chasing the British army down to the docks, firing at them, and the last British officer would be backing up the gangway onto the boat with his pistol in his hand.' The IRA knew that's what had happened four years before in Aden in 1967 – although it was an aeroplane the fleeing British boarded – but the seventeen-year-old Bradley and his contemporaries saw direct comparisons.

What did he do in those frantic days? Planted bombs and fired at

British soldiers, police and loyalists whenever he had the chance, which was almost every day. The IRA company he was in would have been involved in at least three or four operations a day. '"Operation" is too grand a word. You got a weapon, fired five to ten shots, gave it to a girl: she bolted. No question of washing off residues or anything like that. Forensics didn't come into it then. Just shoot and walk away. We didn't know about forensics. Neither did the Brits. It was just blatter, blatter, blatter, and walk away. Maybe go into a bar or walk into a house. Never think of washing, as you would in the eighties. No great pre-planning. Ops were done in minutes.

'There had to be some degree of planning, of course, even makeshift. People weren't just walking around with guns. You saw an opportunity, but you had to get the gear and you could miss your chance. You had to plan a run back, how to get the weapon away. And a girl didn't just pop up. She was as much part of the op as the guy who fired. You had to know where she was: in the next street, in a house, standing fifty yards away round a corner. She had to know what to do, where to run. When you gave her the gun, she knew to bolt in a different direction from you. So it was arranged beforehand as much as possible.

'That's why Armalites were so useful, because the stock folded. Same with Peter the Painter. The girl could stuff it down her front or under her frock. It was rare for women soldiers to be in a foot patrol and the girl couldn't be searched if it was only men. Still, they could hold the girl or take her off to the barracks to be searched.' Bradley reels off the names of three women caught with guns, one with an Armalite.

Of course, like every other youth in Unity Flats, Bradley was arrested a few times, but released after being searched and questioned. He had no weapon and denied everything. No forensic tests were done on him. But his charmed existence couldn't last. After the unionist-inspired fiasco of internment, the British army were now firmly in charge and were building up their own intelligence. They began to create a profile of every person in nationalist working-class districts across the city. They regularly 'lifted' males for 'screening', that is, holding them for four hours to check out if their stories about their identity, their address, their background stood up. Many were gratuitously beaten, partly *pour encourager les autres*, partly because their interrogators thought they had some information, partly as some soldiers vented their frustrations about friends and colleagues being killed and injured. Whatever the pretext, beatings were routine.

In January 1972, Bradley's luck ran out. Along with another IRA member, John Moore, he was in a car going to meet a girl in Ardoyne. Ardoyne was the most comfortable place for north Belfast IRA men to socialise because it was the biggest, safest district in the third battalion area. There was overwhelming support from the people because of the horrifying experiences in 1969, when streets of houses were burnt and people shot dead, and now in 1971 because of continual loyalist attacks and the depredations of British soldiers. Due to the intense hostility of people in Ardoyne towards them, the British army generally operated only on the periphery of the district, unless they made an incursion in force specifically to try to arrest an individual. Like all the other nationalist enclaves in Belfast, Ardoyne still had barricades at each entrance and IRA lookouts who would warn of loyalist or army incursions by blowing whistles or rattling metal dustbin lids.

The car with Moore and Bradley in it was stopped by the British army on the edge of Ardoyne. Stupidly, because they were not on an IRA operation, the car had false number plates, which, of course, did not check out when the army patrol radioed in. Bradley was taken to Girdwood barracks, the main army base in north Belfast; then came the most frightening experience of his young life. He remembers being taken into a large room, perhaps fifteen metres by ten. Around the walls were about forty cubicles, separated from each other by a partition, one and a half metres high. Men were sitting on chairs in the cubicles, facing the wall in silence. 'The atmosphere was horrible. As soon as you went in, you were hit. I saw a man from Unity Flats I recognised, a big tough guy and said, "Will you tell my ma I'm here?" The guy looked terrified and whispered, "You're not allowed to speak here."

'Every so often soldiers or police would take a man out for questioning. They all got beaten. The main man doing the beatings was a Scottish man. I remember he was called Seumas. You could hear men squealing. Some of the policemen were drunk and lashed out at people for no reason. I particularly recall Paddy Fitzsimmons, [a former member of the Irish Olympic boxing team], being repeatedly beaten and dragged back into the hall, unconscious. I reckon Fitzsimmons was practically unconscious for forty-eight hours.' Fitzsimmons was interned and later took his case to the European Court of Human Rights.

As for Bradley, he only got slapped, as he says, in Girdwood – that is to say, hit around the head and face with an open hand. Despite successfully maintaining that he knew nothing, the game was up. His run of luck was over. He could deny everything, as he did, but others under interrogation at different locations were going to name him as a prolific gunman. He was not released. The next he knew, he was on his way to the prison ship HMS *Maidstone*, moored in Belfast Lough.

4

BLOODY FRIDAY AND OPERATION MOTORMAN

'People would be assigned the day before the op, or even
on the morning. There'd be mad rushing around, opening dumps,
getting guns – all shorts for the bombing teams. G company was
well organised and very experienced at bombing.'

The period from August 1971 to the end of 1974 marked the peak
of intensity of the IRA's campaign, with 1972 the most violent year,
when 497 people were killed, including 108 British soldiers and
259 civilians. Nearly a hundred people were killed in the month of
July alone. It is said there were 'over' ten thousand shooting incidents, though how anyone could keep an accurate record is questionable. The British army also recorded 1,382 explosions that
year. Both shootings and explosions tended to be concentrated in
Belfast and Derry, though, of course, there were horrific incidents
in many other places such as Claudy, a small rural town where nine
people were killed by a bomb in July. Alongside the carnage, there

was seismic political turmoil in the North as British governments from 1971 to 1974 struggled to find a political path to end the horrendous violence, though by 1974 many British politicians had despaired of a resolution and talked of settling for 'an acceptable level of violence'.

With the IRA campaign going at full pelt, these years, naturally, marked the high point of the military careers of combatants like Gerry Bradley. They would never again experience the same constant adrenalin rush, the same belief that every action advanced the cause of a united Ireland, the same certainty that the campaign was going to succeed within a foreseeable timescale if operations could be kept going at the same frenetic rate. Bradley's career followed the same trajectory as that of hundreds of other IRA volunteers: headlong, reckless shooting and bombing in these years to keep the British under pressure, inevitable capture and internment, followed by a plateau of much-reduced activity and then the long, slow, gradual rundown of IRA activity in the 1980s to the 1994 ceasefire.

Unlike many others who walked away for a variety of reasons, Bradley was one of the minority who kept coming back after each stint in prison, always anxious to up the ante, to increase the frequency of operations, to return somehow to the pace of the years 1971-74, which had put the British on the back foot. Why did he keep coming back? 'Rebel heart. The British army were there. They were on our streets – arrogant. They shouldn't be here. No, it wasn't the buzz of operations. There was that. But if you believe it, you believe it. The IRA was a vehicle for getting at the Brits, the best one available. It could have been the IRB, or IR something else, but the IRA was the best and the only vehicle around in 1969. For a long time I really did believe, first, we could drive the Brits into the sea and then, later, that we could beat them down and weaken them, sicken them, so that they'd have to negotiate and that they'd give up on the unionists. Well, that did happen, to an extent.

'As for the guys who jacked it in, they had lots of reasons: family reasons, under pressure from wives, fear of doing time if they were caught again after a previous conviction, just getting older, having a row with somebody in the 'RA, or they just felt they'd done their bit.

'Some guys thought it wasn't going anywhere. If they'd done their bit and done their time, you couldn't criticise them. You could argue about the point of carrying on, all right. I thought they were wrong, and told them, but you weren't gonna change their mind and they weren't gonna change mine. Even if they didn't come back, most still continued to help out. There were lots of guys like me, though, who came back after doing years. One guy from Unity must have done sixteen years altogether, that's the equivalent of a thirty-two-year sentence. I did nothing near that. So I'm not the only one, by any means.'

Unknown to Bradley and the physical force men like him, who placed all their faith in the armed struggle, for much of this time both the IRA leadership and various British governments were looking for a way to end the campaign. In August 2006, Gerry Kelly told a BBC programme, reflecting on the British army's analysis of the conflict, that 'the IRA sued for peace twice'; that is to say, they formally approached the British offering a ceasefire on certain conditions and asking for negotiations. One of those occasions was in 1972, at the height of the violence.

The IRA made their offer, as they believed, from a position of strength in early summer 1972. The rate of shootings and bombings soared exponentially after internment and peaked in the months after 30 January 1972, 'Bloody Sunday', when British paratroopers shot and killed thirteen unarmed civilians in Derry and wounded many others, one of whom died from his wounds. It was self-evident that internment had not served the purpose the Stormont government had asserted it would, and, as events on the streets went from bad to awful, the British government abolished the unionist regime in March 1972. The British had decided to run Northern Ireland directly from Westminster. A senior British politician, Willie Whitelaw, was appointed as Secretary of State for Northern Ireland, with a brief to bring an end to the conflict.

One of Whitelaw's early actions, to try to improve the overall climate, was to deal with the disastrous effects of internment. He immediately began to release internees. Within a month of his appointment, he had released over two hundred. Obviously, the younger inmates, about whose detention there had been much adverse publicity, got priority. One of them was Gerry Bradley, set free a fortnight after his eighteenth birthday. Bradley's first stint of internment had lasted five months, until May 1972.

Teenage internees, like Bradley, on the *Maidstone* quickly came to the avuncular attention of Kevin Hannaway, a veteran republican and uncle of Gerry Adams, interned in the 1950s. He knew the ropes. Bradley refers to him as 'old Kevin Hannaway' and, on reflection, believes Hannaway must have been in his forties then; but to seventeen-year-old Bradley he seemed old. Hannaway knew Bradley's family, of course, because of his republican background and inducted the new internee into the ways of the *Maidstone*.

Bradley recalls how just after he arrived on the ship, a hunger strike was held in protest at the British army killings on Bloody Sunday, January 1972. It lasted three days. 'I was only on the ship and straight in at the deep end. It was terrible. Me and another kid were starving after two days. After three days we couldn't wait for it to be over. Hannaway said: "Now, don't be going at the food when it's over. Take it easy because you're full of wind. Your stomach won't like it." We were just wild with hunger. As soon as we were allowed to eat, we went for it. Of course, Hannaway was right. We were rolling about on our bunks in agony. The pain of the wind was terrible.

'I got visits from my mother and my sister, Mary. They came every week and brought food parcels. When you got a visit, they led you down the gangplank to Portakabins with tables and chairs in them. My mother said it was like when she was a wee girl visiting her uncle on the *Argenta* [a prison ship in Belfast harbour in 1922], history repeating itself.

'The worst thing about it all was not knowing how long it was going to last. The older men talked in terms of years. But guys were being released all the time for no rhyme or reason, and this preyed on people's minds. Soon, I was out too. I never knew why. I was only in a few months and never had to come to grips with it all.'

On his release from internment, Bradley immediately reported back to the OC of his district and asked for a week off before going into action again. According to the official British military analysis of their army's campaign in the North, Bradley's was exactly the route followed by at least 60 percent of men released from internment in 1972: they went straight back into the IRA. Thus, by the summer, the new British secretary of state had unwittingly supplied the IRA with a couple of hundred reinforcements, men fired up with resentment at their treatment and a desire to strike back. These men emerged from the internment centres – the *Maidstone* prison ship, Long Kesh and Magilligan – with more training in weaponry and explosives than they possessed before they had been interned, and with a strong sense of camaraderie, of being part of a large organisation stretching across Ireland.

They were released into an IRA vastly better equipped and expanded, compared to six months before. The IRA was going from strength to strength. After internment, then Bloody Sunday, the IRA was inundated with recruits. Membership in Belfast alone in 1972 probably exceeded 1,500, which explains why north Belfast's third battalion had expanded from three to seven companies by spring 1972. IRA members were convinced they were winning. They had brought down Stormont, and IRA operations across the North were running at an increasing tempo, often in excess of a hundred a day. In April 1972 alone, the IRA detonated 2,000 kilograms of explosives compared to 100 kilograms in April 1971.

The main ingredient of the explosives for IRA bombs was ammonium nitrate, readily available in large quantities around the countryside as fertiliser. Marketed as Net Nitrate, it was the most commonly used fertiliser in Ireland. The Irish government had shares in Net Nitrate. Every farm in the country had bags of the stuff lying around.

'They brought it into Belfast from the country in the North and in the Republic in plastic bags. It was usually hidden in the doors of cars and vans. There was so much "mix", as we called it, coming into Belfast to be made into bombs that Belfast IRA members developed a skin rash from handling it every day.

'We had a house full of it in the Docks. An old guy lived there and he didn't care. Every room was full. We had to move it, not because he complained, but you could actually smell it from across the street. You know that marzipan smell that comes from it? Any Brit patrol would've known immediately.

'The rash was a real problem. Half of G company had it. We had to get it dealt with quick because Belfast Brigade was afraid in case IRA bomb-makers could be identified by the skin rash and lifted. Some guys had to go south until it cleared. It was a hospital consultant, a sympathiser, solved the problem for us. We didn't know that if you were handling the mix you needed a well-ventilated, preferably open-air space, otherwise particles got under your skin and into mucous membranes and caused irritation and runny nose and eyes.' Knowing that was one thing; unfortunately, the consultant could not solve the problem of finding well-ventilated spaces for making bombs.

Not only was there an unlimited supply of explosives, Bradley was thrilled to find that the weaponry had improved dramatically. When Bradley was arrested, the IRA in north Belfast had been depending on old British army Lee Enfield .303 rifles and shotguns and the occasional Thompson sub-machine gun. On release, he was delighted to find these had been relegated to 'defence gear' for use as a last resort by auxiliaries, and that the Belfast IRA now had access to some modern SLR rifles, stolen from British soldiers, but, most importantly, to two hundred modern American Armalite AR-18 rifles. These weapons weighed only three kilograms, fired a high velocity round and had a folding stock that made them ideal for hiding under a coat or a skirt, or in the bottom of a pram. They had been brought across the Atlantic on the *QE2* liner from New York. Irish-American longshoremen had shipped them in the hold to Southampton. Gabriel McGahey from Ardoyne, later to be one of the IRA's main gunrunners in the USA, lived in Southampton. He and another Belfast man, Liam Baker, organised the shipment of the weapons to Belfast docks where seamen, sympathetic to the IRA, brought them ashore. Bradley says the seamen simply slung the weapons over their shoulders in canvas duffle bags, two at a time, with stocks folded, and walked out of the docks home.

The IRA also had access to what Bradley describes as 'good old stuff like Mausers' – indeed, his favourite weapon was 'good old stuff', a type of Mauser nicknamed 'Peter the Painter' after Peter Piatkov, a Latvian revolutionary who made the model famous in a stand-off in London in 1911, which the press of the time called the 'Siege of Sidney Street'. The gun was ideal for close-quarter urban gun battles. It was a semi-automatic pistol, and had a detachable wooden shoulder stock that doubled as a holster. For Bradley, it had the added cachet that it was the same model that Patrick Pearse had used and surrendered to the British army in 1916 and is now displayed in the museum in Collins barracks in Dublin.

In 2007, when Bradley learnt of this exhibition, he and a companion travelled to Dublin to see it. The verdict was, 'brilliant'. 'We went through all the rooms and we read all the stuff in the room about Pearse and the 'Tan war. We came home on the train more convinced than ever that we had been doing the right thing.'

The model Bradley used fired a long 9mm parabellum round, a couple of millimetres longer than modern 9mm cartridges. The long rounds were difficult to procure, but the utility of the weapon outweighed that disadvantage. The gun was easy to conceal; it was accurate, reliable, and the detachable stock extended its effective range to 800 metres. Bradley recalls, 'That gun done some damage in Unity.' It was eventually lost in the New Lodge to a British army search.

Still, despite the influx of weaponry into Belfast, there was always a shortage for local units. The increasing frequency of British army searches meant that the policy of IRA quartermasters was 'the more you give, the more you lose.' Therefore, highly prized weapons, like Armalites, were kept for important operations. As a result, there was intense competition within and between companies to get access to guns. Bradley, who in June 1972 became assistant quartermaster to G company, spent a lot of time with the quartermaster, his friend and IRA mentor 'Blue' Kelly, trying to acquire Armalites from the Belfast Brigade. They managed to get two. IRA companies usually went into action with a hotchpotch of weaponry, some modern, some, like the Peter the Painter, dating back to World War I. People were queuing up to have a shot at the army and there were objections to individuals 'hogging' weapons, with men pleading: C'mon, give us a go; you got shooting yesterday.

The gun battles were not confined to exchanges with the British army. From August 1971 there was increasing activity by loyalist organisations like the UVF and the newly emerged UDA. Both organisations were given to random attacks on Catholics. A hundred metres from the western end of Unity Flats, a new social housing complex of flats was being built to house Protestants from the lower Shankill, who had complained bitterly about being overlooked for new housing as the Unity complex grew. The new complex facing Unity was built from materials inferior even to that which had gone into Unity. The layout and design of the flats bore all the hallmarks of a rush job: they quickly earned the derisive nickname of 'the Weetabix blocks' because their façade looked like the rectangular breakfast cereal. They were deeply unpopular among Shankill people, who soon refused to take lets in them. Within a decade, they were demolished.

However, while they were being built they provided useful firing points for Shankill Road gunmen. Loyalists in the Weetabix blocks often fired indiscriminately into the Unity complex or at individuals walking about in the open spaces between blocks. As a preventative measure, Bradley and other G company members blazed away at the Weetabix blocks under construction, unable, at a distance of a hundred metres, to distinguish between UVF or UDA gunmen and building workers who were on site at the time; and any firing from the Weetabix blocks was immediately met with a fusillade in reply from Unity's IRA men. 'We used to blatter back every time there was movement.' Eventually, the construction company dropped large tarpaulins the full length of the building in progress so that IRA men in Unity Flats could not see men on the scaffolding or walkways to fire at. No matter: Bradley and his fellow IRA men blazed away at the tarpaulins at random because UDA and UVF gunmen were using them as cover to fire into Unity. Amazingly, despite all that gunfire, no one on either side was killed in these exchanges.

Firing on the British army was incomparably more hazardous. Bradley's friend, Blue Kelly, saved him once when he was caught in crossfire in the open. Bradley and Kelly had fired at members of 40 Marine Commando in a Land Rover as they drove past Unity, a hazard for any military vehicle. Unlike members of other regiments, however, the marines immediately dismounted and gave chase towards the sound of the gunfire. As Bradley and Kelly ran off across open ground littered with debris, Bradley tripped over a brick or a concrete block and crashed to the ground. Immediately the pursuing marines, who had split into two groups, concentrated their fire on him from different directions.

'The Brits were blazing away. There was dirt jumping up all round. I still had hold of the M1 carbine I'd been using, so I knew they knew they'd got an IRA man and if they shot me they'd be within their rights. They'd be cheering. I couldn't use the M1 to fire back because I was so low and keeping my head down. I was real scared they were going to make a job of it. They were getting the range. The bullets were hitting closer: three yards, two yards, ricocheting off the tarmac. The dirt was spitting into my eyes, stinging my face. I was going to be shot dead if I didn't get up and run, but if I did get up I'd be shot too.'

He was pinned down by the marines' accurate fire. He thinks it all lasted for about two minutes. 'It could just as easily have been thirty seconds. It seemed to go on for ages, but it was all over in no time, really.' Blue Kelly ran out from his cover a few yards away, grabbed Bradley by his jeans and dragged him into cover, still holding the M1. Nowadays, Kelly never misses an opportunity to remind Bradley of what he did. Bradley tells Kelly he ran out only because he thought there was the price of a pint in the hip pocket of Bradley's jeans, which he grabbed to pull him to safety.

In the early summer of 1972, such daily gun battles were the norm. If so, why were the IRA so ineffective? Bradley insists that G company inflicted far more casualties than the British admitted – not necessarily fatalities, but, he claims, several soldiers were badly wounded and the army never admitted it. 'I saw soldiers hit and fall. I remember one on the roof of Unity. He was definitely hit. Never a word about it. There were Brits injured by blast bombs too. Unity was so small we tended to use shorts [pistols] not heavy stuff, because you couldn't hide that easily or quickly. You were always careful not to lose weapons. We had good dumps. We didn't just go out and take pot shots and get the whole place swamped. Too risky. We waited our chance. We banked on the fact that Unity was a maze to outsiders. Every door was open to us. You could fire at passing army vehicles and run, disappear between blocks. That time the marines chased us was a one-off. Usually the Land Rover just took off.

'Anyway, G company was more into bombing, being so close to the city centre. We sent bombs into Belfast city centre from Unity on a daily basis.' The bombs had a devastating effect. The Smith-field bus depot, a hundred metres from Unity Flats, was extensively damaged by a 25-kilogram bomb in April, and in May the main Cooperative store in Northern Ireland, two hundred metres from Unity, was destroyed by fire after a bomb exploded. Bradley says that the company OC, 'Big Seán', who had built up G company from the beginning of the year, allowed them 'to do anything'. It was the male members of G who did the shooting and planted the large bombs, 25-50 kilograms carried in suitcases or in the boot of a car. Women members carried the smaller bombs, five to ten kilos, and incendiary devices into town.

But those frenzied days when the Belfast and Derry IRA,

operating from within their barricaded districts, held the initiative, were coming to an end. In June, the IRA offered the British government talks. Though he issued a public rejection of the offer, the new British Secretary of State, Willie Whitelaw, immediately put out secret feelers to the IRA leadership, to try to bring about a ceasefire and some negotiations. All IRA companies were asked to consider a proposed ceasefire. At the G Company meeting, Bradley was one of only two volunteers who disagreed with it. He saw matters from a Unity Flats perspective and, it should be said, from the perspective of someone who had just turned eighteen. He was on a high, in action every day and he believed the IRA could drive the British into the sea. They had the guns, the explosives, the support in the community he operated out of. He thought they should keep going because he believed if they kept up the pressure the British would abandon the unionists. It just wouldn't be worth their while to stay. There was no percentage in it.

Now he admits: 'If the Brits had withdrawn we'd have been in serious shit. At least the Brits took on the IRA. If they'd left, the RUC and UDR would still have had their guns and they'd just have come in to finish the job they started in 1969. There'd have been slaughter. Like, the RUC and UDR had armoured cars and heavy weapons. How were the Brits going to disarm them before they left? They weren't. In those days I thought if the Brits left, the Unionists would see the game was up and make a deal with the IRA, see it was inevitable. When the Brits left, they would have no option. Most people in the 'RA thought that then.'

He also thought 'the British were trying a tactic to find out who was in the 'RA.' This result had always come out of a ceasefire: previously unknown IRA members would be seen associating with known activists. Also, nobody was sure what the terms of a ceasefire really would be. Would there still be searches, arrests? Could people still be interned? Would British troops still patrol nationalist districts? Would they even abide by the terms of a ceasefire?

Needless to say, Bradley's views counted for nothing. The decision had already been taken at the highest levels in the IRA. On 22 June, the IRA announced that a ceasefire would come into force at midnight on 26 June. In the meantime, Bradley and G company, like other IRA companies across the North, went hell-for-leather to kill or injure as many British soldiers as possible, reaching a crescendo on the evening of 26 June. Despite all their efforts, no soldier was in fact killed in their area during the days leading up to the ceasefire.

It certainly was not for want of trying. On the evening the ceasefire was due to come into effect, fourteen or fifteen members of G company were in action, including Bradley and Blue Kelly. Among other weapons, Bradley remembers, they had a Garand M1 rifle, an M2 which could be fully automatic, a Peter the Painter, an SLR stolen from the army and a Marlin sub-machine gun, which fired .45 inch bullets from a drum magazine. The Marlin was an exotic, prized weapon, a light machine gun with enormous firepower. Blue Kelly had it. It was 'light' only in respect of its calibre, because, in fact, it was heavy and bulky and not designed for being carried while running about in the dark around corners in street fighting.

At one point, Kelly propped it against a wall where he was taking cover, and ran to find out what the rest of the group were up to. It was lucky for him that he had left his position, because no sooner had he moved than British soldiers ran to it to take cover. If he had not moved, he would have been shot or captured: but they stumbled on the gun, no doubt much to their relief and satisfaction. Kelly was desolate.

There was a sequel to this incident two days later. The ceasefire terms allowed senior IRA figures to move about unmolested by the security forces, a freedom the IRA immediately took advantage of to rally their troops and raise morale. As part of this exercise, the IRA chief of staff, Seán Mac Stíofáin, came from Dublin to visit units in Belfast, including the third battalion. There was a large gathering of more than three hundred men and women in what later became the Celtic club in the New Lodge Road.

Mac Stíofáin had no small idea of his own importance. At the time of this meeting, he would have known that he was about to be flown to England with other IRA leaders, including Gerry Adams and Martin McGuinness, to meet the North's British Secretary of State, Willie Whitelaw. The summer of 1972 was the high point of Mac Stíofáin's career in Irish republican politics and the IRA, a career which up to that time had lasted over twenty years, including eight years in Wormwood Scrubs prison for a failed weapons raid on a British army barracks in England in the 1950s. In July 1972 he was in his full majesty, leading the largest number of IRA combatants since 1922.

He did not go down well in the New Lodge Road Celtic Club. Bradley found him 'uppity and obnoxious, full of himself'. Mac Stíofáin had received a report about the battalion's recent actions, including the loss of the Marlin, which, of course, was an offence under IRA rules. Mac Stíofáin called over Big Seán, G company's OC, and told him Blue Kelly was 'dismissed from the army' for losing the Marlin, a prestige weapon. Big Seán came back to his G company men and told them what Mac Stíofáin had said. Kelly was stunned. Bradley says Kelly almost burst into tears. The IRA was his life. And to Bradley and many others in G company, Kelly was a hero. 'For the New Lodge and Unity, he was the equivalent of Dan Breen. A Belfast Brigade Active Service Unit (ASU) of top operators had been set up in 1971 and he was in it. He was brilliant at ops. He was brilliant at getting gear.' Everybody looked at each other in amazement at Mac Stíofáin's decision. After a short discussion among themselves, the company said, 'No way.' Big Seán went back to Mac Stíofáin and told him, 'Dismiss Blue and the whole company's walking.' Blue stayed and in the following years, right into the 1980s, would play a major part in organising weapons and explosives shipments from Libya, getting on good personal terms with Colonel Gaddafi and one of his many sons, who, by all accounts, regarded Kelly as a close personal friend.

A week or so after the Mac Stíofáin visit – and to Bradley's relief – the ceasefire collapsed on 9 July amid mutual recriminations between the British army and the IRA. It was back to 'business'. The IRA was planning to step up its operations and immediately did so, but the British government had already decided that the rising curve of IRA activity could not be allowed to continue. Plans had been laid in late 1971 to bring an end to the barricaded so-called NOGO areas in Belfast and Derry, where IRA teams planned and launched operations with impunity. The problem for the British was that taking control of the NOGO areas could lead to death and injury among the civilian populations of those areas. In the aftermath of the killings on Bloody Sunday, such an outcome could make matters inconceivably worse and inflame international opinion. There had to be some pretext for such a major military operation and, luckily for the British, the IRA were unwittingly about to provide it.

The IRA had been planning its own major operation. It proved to be a catastrophic mistake and became known as 'Bloody Friday'. On the afternoon of 21 July, the Belfast Brigade exploded twenty bombs across Belfast in just over an hour, killing nine people and injuring 130, among them seventy-seven women and children. Seán Mac Stíofáin demonstrated how little grip he had on reality by trying to explain that the bombs were 'a concerted sabotage offensive', to show the IRA was strong enough to carry out a large number of simultaneous attacks. He blamed the British for failing to pass on IRA phone warnings about the location of the bombs, a line which remained the official IRA explanation for years afterwards. Thirty years later, the IRA issued an apology for the deaths and injuries inflicted that day.

The Belfast IRA leaders knew immediately that they faced a

major strategic crisis in the aftermath of the bombs. The irresponsible targeting and the indiscriminate killings and injuries had handed the British a major propaganda victory. It looked as though the IRA was engaged in a campaign of wholesale and arbitrary terror, far from pinpoint attacks on the Crown forces and the North's economy, as they claimed. One former senior Belfast IRA figure, Brendan 'Darkie' Hughes, said in 1997: 'What happened on Bloody Friday was a disaster. It was largely the fault of the IRA. I think they overestimated the British army's capabilities of clearing that particular area that day and it resulted in that disaster.'

Gerry Adams wrote in his book *Before the Dawn*: 'It is clear that the IRA made a mistake in putting out so many bombs, and civilians were killed who should not have been killed. This was the IRA's responsibility and a matter of deep regret.' His book was published in 1996. Twenty-four years earlier, Adams was not saying anything in public, but he was reportedly furious with the consequences of the bombing. At the time, Adams was adjutant or second-in-command to Seamus Twomey, OC of the Belfast Brigade. Adams had played no part in the initial planning of the major demonstration of IRA strength in Belfast, since he was in Long Kesh when the bomb blitz was devised. However, when the plan was resurrected in July after the collapse of the ceasefire, Adams would have been fully aware of the operation, since he had been released to help negotiate the ceasefire and then became adjutant of the Belfast Brigade. The twelve days between the end of the ceasefire and the bombings would have been taken up with finalising plans for the operation. Gerry Bradley says it is inconceivable that Adams was not aware: 'If an ADJ [adjutant] says he doesn't know what's going on, it's like a TV director saying he doesn't know what his producer is planning. An ADJ has to know everything in case the OC's lifted. He takes over. That's what he's for' – though the operation had been decided while Adams was interned and there was no way he could have stopped it. Seamus Twomey was adamant and, anyway, MacStíofáin wanted a big spectacular.

Bradley says the strategy of the concerted bombings which turned into Bloody Friday 'came from the very top. Mac Stíofáin and Dublin okayed it all.' The overall planning, however, was down to the Belfast Brigade, whose operations officer handed a lot of the detailed action to the third battalion, the one covering Bradley's district. The third battalion put out eleven of the twenty bombs that exploded that afternoon, a huge logistical exercise involving dozens of men and women: selecting targets, stealing and preparing cars to carry bombs or act as getaway vehicles, planning escape routes, releasing weapons, allocating over 200 kilograms of explosives in fifteen- and twenty-five-kilogram bombs to the various teams, making warning phone calls – including, stupidly, at least two hoax warning calls that sent emergency services careering off on false errands. The whole operation had to be timed for completion in very short order, because the point the IRA leadership wanted to make was the number of bombs they could explode almost simultaneously in Belfast.

One of the major causes for the disaster that ensued was that, incredibly, in 1972 the IRA members planting the bombs had no control over the priming, in many cases not even any precise knowledge of the timing on the bomb fuse. They received the bombs ready-primed from the explosives officer. It was hair-raising stuff. As Bradley says: 'In those days a lot depended on the EO. There were good EOs and not so good. This was before electronics. Often it was a fuse you lit. Like, the EO would have a roll of, say, 100 feet of fuse. He would cut off a bit and see how long it took to burn. Different rolls took different times, often. Then the EO would cut off that length and attach it to the bomb. He'd give you the bomb and say, "When you light this, it's ten minutes, or two minutes, or whatever." Could be thirty seconds on a blast bomb. That's a long time. A nail bomb was five to ten seconds. Couldn't be precise.' It was hardly rocket science.

Even worse, sometimes there was a clockwork timer on the bomb instead of a fuse to be lit. If that was the case, then there was no turning back if passersby were spotted or the bomb team could not reach the intended target because of a checkpoint or traffic hold-up. The bomb was going to explode. The bomb team had to leave it and make off, or they would be killed. If they had to leave it in the 'wrong' place, usually another member of the company was already ringing in the warning and did not know the bomb was in a different place. 'Hoax' calls were not always deliberate hoaxes. They described where the bomb should have been.

All seven companies in the third battalion were in action on Bloody Friday, as well as companies from west Belfast's huge second battalion. IRA officers at company level had only two days' notice or less of the operation. Bomb teams had even shorter notice, sometimes hours, about the location of the bombs they were to plant. Inevitably, some companies were scrabbling around to find teams, even though there were usually only two in a team. Some teams planted two bombs. Some teams were more incompetent or careless than others about the consequences.

'The way it would work was this: the brigade operations officer would meet the battalion OCs and brief them about the big op. The battalion OCs would then meet their company OCs and ask them had they any ops planned, any near ready to go. An OC might have half a dozen ops on the shelf at any one time, maybe as many as ten waiting for the opportunity, the weapons, the explosives. Then the battalion OC would ask the company OC: "How many of them can you do tomorrow? How many can you do between two o'clock and three o'clock?"

'People would be assigned the day before the op, or even on the morning. There'd be mad rushing around, opening dumps, getting guns – all shorts [pistols] for the bombing teams. G company was well organised and very experienced at bombing. Big Seán, the OC, would say to a couple of volunteers, "We need a four-door." Then, after they stole the car or hijacked it, the car would have to be brought back for the bomb team, or maybe brought to collect the bomb, and then the bomb team would take over. The bomb team was usually two, the driver and a man with a gun.

'You had to be very aggressive when you were the man with the gun, shouting, scaring people into believing it was the real thing – because it was – making them run, making sure there was no resistance. All our bombs were designed to destroy economic targets, and they did. Nobody got injured and all IRA volunteers returned safely.'

Bradley played a full part in the Bloody Friday operations. G company, being close to the city centre, put out four bombs, more than any other company in the battalion, including one which destroyed Smithfield bus depot and another planted in a garage in Donegall Street, near the offices of the *Irish News*, the North's main nationalist newspaper, which the bomb badly damaged.

G company's John Moore drove the car to the garage on Donegall Street, accompanied by another volunteer in the passenger seat armed with a .45 revolver. They carried the bomb into the garage and shouted a warning. As often happened, some of the garage workers did not believe them. Moore's partner 'had to kick one guy up the backside and force him out. As they came out after planting the bomb, two jeeps of military police pulled up just beside where their getaway car was parked ten yards away. The MPs were carrying Sterling sub-machine guns. Moore and his mate just walked by them, got into the car and away, shitting themselves. Or, as the IRA statement would say, "the ASU returned safely to base."'

Once G company's four bombs were planted, Bradley and Big Seán went up to the top floor of one of the twelve-storey blocks of flats in the New Lodge to watch the bombs exploding across Belfast. As they watched the black palls of smoke rising and heard the deep rumble and boom of the explosions, and listened to the wail of the ambulance and fire brigade sirens for the next hour, they had no anticipation of the ramifications of the day's events for the IRA's strategy. It was only when the casualty toll began to rise that realisation sank in what a bloody mess the whole exercise had been.

'For all the work we put in to make sure our people were safe and no one got hurt, when the casualty figures starting coming in, it was a real dampener. The best thing is doing an op, getting out, getting home. The civilians being killed ruined everything. On the Friday morning I thought "brilliant", we're perfectly organised. On the Friday night I thought "disaster" – not in a military way, but because of all the mistakes and deaths. I remember sitting watching TV news with my mother. She watched the pictures and said, "God bless us."

'You had to explain to supporters next day and next week what happened – about road checks blocking bomb cars getting to their targets, having to leave them because the timer was running, and then warning calls about where they should have been, all that. You had to explain, because people were letting you use their houses, but they knew we weren't going out deliberately to kill people all round us. It just turned out a mess.'

The widespread condemnation in all the electronic and print media, British and Irish, of the bombings and their enormous civilian casualties, gave the British government a cast-iron reason to implement Operation Motorman, their code name for taking control of the NOGO areas. The date was set for 31 July, ten days after the carnage of Bloody Friday. Days before the operation was to be mounted, the British deliberately signalled their intentions in the hope that the IRA would not organise any serious resistance, as indeed was the case.

The British army reinforced their troops in the North of Ireland with four thousand extra men, deployed Centurion tanks with bulldozer attachments in Derry, and heavy, six-wheeled Saladin armoured cars in Derry and Belfast to demolish the barricades at the entrance to hard-line republican districts. With twelve thousand troops deployed, it was the biggest military exercise the British army had engaged in since Suez. Wisely, like any guerrilla army, the IRA melted away into their homes and safe houses in the face of overwhelming odds.

'Motorman was really a Derry thing, breaking into Free Derry and all that. That's where they used the tank. You couldn't have done anything where we were either. There weren't any orders not to resist, but there was no need for orders. We were out rioting, throwing everything at them, but the Brits came in that strong it would've been madness to take out a gun in Unity. Shooting at them would have been just silly. You'd have lost weapons and maybe even dumps. You'd have got the whole place wrecked. I do remember a big woman MP [military police] – a monster, huge – chasing us. The women out banging the bin lids ran. I ran. I wasn't going to get arrested for throwing bricks.'

Breaking into republican enclaves was only the beginning. The British army was there to stay. Much to the fury of the nationalist population, the soldiers took over schools, halls, recreation centres, playing fields, GAA grounds – anywhere they could billet troops and park vehicles securely. They quickly built fortified observation posts, sand-bagged posts called 'sangars', at many street corners and on top of buildings. The aim was to dominate republican districts, prevent movement by IRA members, put an end to the ability to transport arms and explosives around and into Belfast, and to prevent a repetition of anything like Bloody Friday.

The heavy military presence also put an end to the regular gun battles between the British army and IRA, which had rattled round republican districts in 1972. This was particularly true in the case of G company's area of operations. Bradley says: 'Unity Flats was too small. It was easily sealed off. That's what immediately happened now after a shooting. The Brits were on the spot. Weapons could be lost. Shootings were seriously restricted after Motorman.'

The changed circumstances can be illustrated by the fate of Marine David Allan. He was shot dead five days before Operation Motorman in the sort of operation that became a rarity after Motorman. The marine was standing at the corner of Unity Walk and Upper Library Street as his patrol waited for an Orange march from the Shankill Road to pass the flats complex. As Marine Allan stood at the corner, an IRA sniper, firing a Luger pistol, at a range of twenty-five metres, from the top floor of the block of flats behind him, shot him in the head. The same bullet travelled on to clip another marine nearby on the chin, badly injuring him. Bradley says: 'It wasn't something the IRA planned, it was pure spur-of-the-moment. The marines were a target of opportunity. They were in Unity. You could get the gear and get away.'

After Motorman there was a sangar on the corner twenty metres from where those marines had been standing. There was another on the next corner five metres along from that one. Henceforth, it would be madness to use the block of flats from which the shot had been fired that killed Marine Allan. The flats would have been instantly cordoned off and each flat searched. Even if the sniper was not identified or arrested, almost certainly the weapon would have been lost. Then again, Marine Allan would not have been standing in the open, but manning the fortified sangar. Everything changed after Motorman.

Also, two weeks before Motorman, in frustration at a low-flying helicopter clattering incessantly over Unity Flats in the middle of July 1972, Bradley and another G company member fired a couple of rifle shots at it. A pilot did actually report hearing one shot, which caused no damage to his aircraft. A fortnight later, that sort of action would have brought immediate reaction from the dozens of marines stationed in and around the flats after Operation Motorman. Incidentally, it was only after he had fired the shots that it occurred to Bradley what a disaster it would have been for the people of Unity if he had managed to down the helicopter on top of them.

'It took us a while to get used to it all. The army hoisted in dragon's teeth [pyramidal concrete tank traps] to block all the exits and entrances to Unity, except one. So if you were driving in or out, you had only one route. Made it very difficult to get stuff in or out.

You also had to pass the army sangar on foot, so people were stopped regularly.

'We had to watch and wait. Spot their routines. Having troops there twenty-four/seven meant any ops had to be better planned. No spur-of-the-moment stuff. We had to change tactics. You know, like the US Marines' "Adapt and overcome". We had to work out their blind spots. We used the dragon's teeth against them – we fired from behind them at the sangars. They were brilliant as firing points for resting the gun on and, of course, they were bullet-proof. The dragon's teeth also meant the army couldn't get their vehicles in or out either, except through the same one way, so we knew that's where to be ready to throw blast bombs or have a shot.

'Any op in Unity meant raiding parties looking for the weapon. They called it "conducting a search", but it was a raid. Mostly they weren't looking for anything. It was to intimidate and to punish people and make them blame the IRA. In fact, it did the opposite. When raiding parties came in, it was the women who went out to fight them because they knew the Brits were going to wreck their homes. Women would bang bin lids on the ground and get women from all over the district. They'd stand up to the soldiers, throw stuff, slap them.

'The men stayed inside. The soldiers would kick the door in – sometimes they used a sledgehammer if they couldn't kick it in. They would be shouting and yelling, like in a frenzy. They just destroyed things. They ripped seats, broke up chairs, kicked in the TV, threw stuff around, broke windows. They always smashed up the kitchen. They would use the sledge to break the mantelpiece, even the table. They ripped up floorboards, pulled down ceilings, knocked holes in walls. It was real stupid. The women went crazy. Like, they were supposed to blame the IRA's op for the raid?'

Nevertheless, the perpetual presence of the British army after July 1972 did mark the end of a phase where the IRA had the initiative. A place as small as Unity became too hot to use as a base for serious operations. Despite the wanton destruction by British troops, they would also find weapons and explosives. It became too risky to store much in Unity Flats. Battalion meetings and planning too had to shift to the nearby New Lodge or, preferably, Ardoyne. There was an immediate and permanent drop in the number of shootings and bombings in the whole of Belfast, and never again did they reach the huge figures of the first six months of 1972.

5

IN COMMAND

'There was a lot of jealousy and back-stabbing. I suppose there is in any
organisation. Other people wanted to be battalion OC. You got this
constant begrudging, people running, complaining – politics,
I suppose. I just wanted to get on with the biz.'

In August 1972 the British army had twenty-two battalions in the
North, more men than were normally garrisoned in Britain itself.
Many of them had been brought in temporarily from the British
army on the Rhine to implement Operation Motorman, bringing
the total number of troops for a short period to 21,000. Apart from
big bases like Ballykinlar near Newcastle on the County Down
coast, Thiepval at Lisburn and Palace barracks at Hollywood, these
reinforcements were billeted in and around nationalist districts.
After the removal of the barricades in Derry and Belfast, a few
thousand men were immediately withdrawn to take up their
NATO duties again, but a huge presence remained – three battalions in the Lower Falls district alone. The period from summer

1972 to summer 1974 represents the high-water mark of British troop numbers during the Troubles.

The same period also marks the last time the IRA tried to take on the British army as a copycat army organised in traditional units: companies, battalions and brigades. It was just too easy for British military intelligence officers to understand the mechanics of the IRA's structure, draw up lists of the membership of each IRA unit, its area of operations and its command staff, and gradually round them up and throw them all into Long Kesh. Besides, those large IRA units were quickly to prove too easy to infiltrate and subvert. By the end of 1974 there were more senior IRA men inside Long Kesh than outside. One of them was Gerry Bradley.

The domination of hard-line republican districts by large numbers of soldiers was the visible evidence of a very obvious change in British policy after the abortive peace talks in June. There was constant foot-patrolling, backed up by incessant circling in small Ferret armoured cars and mobile patrols in Humber armoured personnel carriers, known as 'pigs', daily arrest operations and house searches, sometimes involving cordoning off whole streets. Although internees continued to be released – over seven hundred by the end of August 1972 – the British government was busily devising a new security policy which would be tied to special courts and allow 'detention orders' and 'interim custody orders' to be made against suspects – internment by another name. The compilation of a vast database began, with all males in republican areas stopped, searched and 'screened' – held up for four hours and their name, address, date of birth, close relatives, occupation, car registration number all noted and cross-referenced. The British government had decided to crush the IRA.

The crazy, helter-skelter days of shooting and bombing at will were over forever. In this new hostile climate, with the oppressive twenty-four hour military presence in their heartlands, the rate of attrition in the IRA grew rapidly. It was quite remarkable that Gerry Bradley lasted eighteen months in effect 'on the run'. In 1972 Bradley was leading the same sort of life as described by Brendan Hughes, a former OC of the Belfast Brigade, in an interview in 1997. Hughes said: 'You would have had a call-house meeting [a safe meeting place] and you might have robbed a bank in the morning, done a float [gone out in a car looking for British soldiers to shoot at] in the afternoon, stuck a bomb and a booby trap out after that, and then maybe had a gun battle or two later that night.'

While Hughes and two or three other teams were engaged in that sort of activity in west Belfast, Bradley and other teams were replicating the operations in north Belfast, though, of course, conditions were much different in the north of the city.

As long as the IRA in west Belfast stayed on their side of the main interface with the Shankill, the whole area was nationalist. Bradley and the others in the third battalion did not have that luxury. The biggest districts they had to operate in were Ardoyne and the New Lodge. Once they emerged from these, there was always the chance of running into a British army or RUC mobile patrol. They had to be rather more careful than Hughes's people in the west. Even so, they carried out the same kind of operations.

'We tried to do something as often as possible. After Motorman you couldn't shoot every day, but *somebody* in the third batt would. It wasn't regular. Maybe one week we'd put out three bombs, the next week one. Maybe rob two banks one week, none the next. Depended on the opportunities. Depended on security presence. Post offices were easier than banks. Shooting at night was easier. Those were the days before the Brits all had night-sights. We just tried to keep it going all the time. No let up.' No wonder Belfast was bedlam in 1972.

By the autumn of 1972, military intelligence officers were developing a picture of IRA personnel. 'Screening', as it was called, was very effective. People were taken and held for four hours. Bradley says: 'If they were satisfied you were who you said you were they asked you about everybody else, virtually nothing about yourself. They pretended they knew all about you; but they knew nothing. They asked about some other guy – who he knocked about with, where he drank, where he worked – all seemingly harmless questions, but they were building a picture, trying to see patterns. People didn't see any harm in answering those questions because they weren't about IRA ops or if the guy was in the IRA. But if the Brits saw this guy somewhere else, with someone else, driving somewhere else, they'd stop him and ask him to explain what he was doing there. If he couldn't, he was in trouble.

'You could answer questions at road checks, okay. Tell them you're going for a drink, tell them anything that fitted. Talk your way out of it. That's different from answering questions in Castlereagh. Orders were not to. Most people did talk, though, and afterwards told the IRA they didn't. But mostly they just talked about football and general rubbish. In the early days there was no training about how to deal with it, but then after internment brought in serious numbers, anti-interrogation lessons were given in the cages in Long Kesh. By the mid-seventies new volunteers were being given instructions because the Labour government had ended internment in 1976 and the aim was to put us all in jail with big sentences.

'There's no doubt the best advice was not to talk about *their* questions because then they came back and started going back over what you'd answered and you got mixed up. I didn't get any of the anti-interrogation training because I was in the army before the whole Castlereagh thing started; so I wasn't "green-booked". I just knew to say nothing.'

Beatings were regular, routine. 'If your story didn't stand up, you got beaten. They knew you were in the 'RA but they couldn't pin anything on you: they didn't have enough to charge you with anything because if they had, they would've charged you. If you got charged, you were going to get a detention order. So, instead, they beat you up and threw you out.' Of course, a lot of youths who weren't in the IRA got beaten up. The behaviour of the troops confirmed nationalists' worst opinions of them. Many men joined, or tried to join, the IRA because of their treatment at the hands of British soldiers.

Other developing techniques British intelligence employed were blackmail, false charges, threats of charges. Men spotted in the wrong place with the wrong woman would be blackmailed, men caught driving without a licence or insurance, drink driving, petty criminals, were all arrested and charged or threatened with charges that would be dropped if they supplied intelligence about IRA members. Bullets were planted on people, or in their cars at road checks. Guns were planted in houses and 'found' during searches. Most damaging of all, IRA members began to give information for money or just to stay out of jail. Pretty soon, British troops knew who the main actors, or 'players' as they began to call them, were in any district.

They didn't know everything. Bradley says: 'There were always "unknowns", that is men who weren't part of IRA structures, didn't want to go into the structure and didn't fit into the normal systems. They were never seen with known IRA men. They carried out specific briefs. One was Terry McIvor, who, for many years, was the main man for explosives and electrics. In the early days he gave all the lectures to the EOs [explosives officers]. He was a lecturer in electronics in a college in Dundalk. He was still advising on bombs and electrical stuff twenty years later.'

But men like McIvor were a rarity. The attrition rate in the IRA was rapid after Operation Motorman, with the British army sitting on their districts. 'Big Seán', G company's OC, was arrested in summer 1972. His successor, John Moore, was shot and badly wounded a few weeks later after a confrontation with a member of the Official IRA, or 'Stickies', the Provisional IRA's nemesis in many Belfast districts (the 'Stickies' were so called because of different Easter Lily badges; the Provisionals used a pin). Moore's replacement, Roger, lasted a few weeks into autumn 1972 before being arrested; then Bradley took his place.

Bradley was eighteen. He now had power over life and death in the area the company controlled. He had about twenty IRA volunteers in the company, mainly from Unity, but a couple from the New Lodge. Altogether, with auxiliaries and Fianna and Cumann na gCailíní, he says he had 'a hundred plus' individuals. The staff usually consisted of an adjutant, quartermaster, finance officer, explosives officer, an intelligence officer and maybe a training officer, abbreviated as FO, EO, IO, TO and so on – 'usually', because people kept getting 'lifted'.

Why was Bradley selected? Obviously, one reason was that the British army had been arresting and interning each company OC in turn. Bradley was next in line to be promoted. It was not so simple, however. There were plenty of eighteen-year-olds around. While that is true, the republican credentials of his family were also a factor. He was of known reliable stock. It is also a fact that he was highly experienced and had developed a formidable reputation since 1969. Bradley was utterly fearless and daring and ruthless: also reckless. He had given himself over completely to the IRA.

He had hijacked vehicles and burnt them. He had been sentenced for riotous behaviour. He had thrown blast bombs and petrol bombs at soldiers and police. He had fired pistols and rifles at soldiers and police in and around Unity Flats. He had helped to plant his first bomb in 1971, aged seventeen, which had successfully blown apart a further-education facility at the bottom of Stanhope Drive in Unity Flats. 'The IRA decided to bomb the place because members of loyalist gangs were signing up to do courses – but they weren't doing any education, just using the place as a base for coming out to attack people from Unity. Nobody was safe walking past it.'

In 1972 he had stopped a unionist mob from the Shankill who were advancing across the waste ground to the rear of Unity Flats. 'There was a whole crowd coming across towards Unity, a good few dozen. They looked as if they meant business. If they got into the back of Unity there was going to be serious fighting, maybe damaging flats, burning. The best thing was to keep them back, stop them getting near. There were enough people from Unity ready to take them on, but the crowd coming would be fighting and doing the damage in our place. I walked out in front of our people and walked towards the Shankill ones so they could see me and the gun. It was a big old British army issue Webley .45 pistol. I crouched down and spread my legs so they could see I was going to fire. I just fired real slow, so they could think about it after every round. I emptied the Webley into them. At that range I probably didn't hit anybody, but it did the job. They scattered.'

As far as people were concerned, that was exactly what the purpose of the IRA in Unity Flats was in 1971 and 1972. People had-confidence in Bradley. By 1972, as IRA activity accelerated,

Bradley had been involved in dozens of shootings and bombings and he had been interned. He had also been a resourceful and successful quartermaster for G company. Quite a CV for an eighteen-year-old, but not completely out of the ordinary in a republican district. Company OC was the next logical step.

Somehow, in the midst of all this IRA activity, he had managed to develop a relationship with a woman, whom he married in December 1972. 'I had to get married from the house of a republican supporter, Teresa McGivern, in the New Lodge district. I'd have been arrested if I'd used my mother's home. The best man was on the run too. It was a pretty low-key wedding, to say the least, in St Patrick's cathedral [a stone's throw from Unity Flats], and the priest was well aware what was at stake. We had a three-day honeymoon in a safe house in Turf Lodge. You couldn't stay anywhere longer. There was no house that safe. That's just the way it was in those days. Loads of people got married like that.

'My sister was married in 1973, but I couldn't go to her wedding or the reception in the Glenshesk Inn at the bottom of Divis Street in case I was 'scooped' [arrested]. Even though it would have been stupid for me to turn up, the army raided the reception to look for me anyway.'

As OC of G company in 1973, Bradley's brief was to up the tempo against the British army. IRA men woke up each morning thinking about what damage they could do. Bradley tried to organise 'something every day, a shooting or a bombing', not easy given the small size and vulnerability of G company's district, in effect,

Unity Flats. He led by example. He says they 'threw loads of blast bombs' from what was known locally as 'Lily Loughran's gap' between two blocks of Unity's flats. They fired 'umpteen times at passing mobile army patrols, at the army sangars in Unity and at soldiers on patrol in Unity. They shot 'repeatedly' from Unity across Clifton Street into Glenravel Street RUC barracks, which doubled as an army base. 'G company didn't hang about. The army sangar at Unity was hit front and back regularly. Brit search parties got a lot of hassle.'

Once, one of the searchers was killed. On 13 November 1972 a four-man patrol from the Queen's regiment had found spent cartridge cases on the ground in Unity Flats and recklessly decided to search adjoining maisonettes in the naive belief that they might find the weapon that fired the shots. Nineteen-year-old Private Stanley Evans was opening a cupboard in the kitchen of a flat when an IRA man outside shot him dead through the kitchen window with a Luger pistol at a range of one and half metres, the same pistol used to kill Marine Allan the previous July.

The IRA's Belfast Brigade issued a statement saying Private Evans was shot in retaliation for the killing of an unarmed IRA man, Stanislaus Carberry, in west Belfast earlier that day. Bradley says that, in fact, the Unity shooting was completely opportunistic, done in a fraction of a second. 'The Brits were in Unity and we could get the gear.' The four-man army patrol was too small to operate for any length of time on its own in Unity's maze of balconies and stairways, and was therefore vulnerable to attack, unable to engage in any follow-up action and forced to call for reinforcements, by which time the gunman was well away and the weapon beyond reach.

Bradley watched the follow-up searches by British troops. An IRA friend advised Bradley to go home and get ready to be arrested next day, because it was inevitable, and best get it over and done with. Next morning, the army raided his mother's house, where he still lived, at about 5.30. She confronted the soldiers and insisted on them letting him have his breakfast, which they did. Bradley says he tried to act cool and unconcerned as he forced down the food, but he knew he was in trouble. His mother had bought him a new jacket for the winter with a fake fur collar and she made him put that on as the soldiers took him from the house. He lit a cigarette and walked out to the Land Rover as casually as he could, climbed in and sat down. The Land Rover hadn't gone five metres when the soldier opposite him hit him a terrific punch in the face. Then the others 'all hit and battered' him. They took him across the road to Glenravel Street barracks and hustled him straight down the stairs to the kitchens, where he was given a bad beating. 'You always knew you were going to get a beating when they took you down to the basement. Nobody could hear you yelling down there.' As well as being kicked and punched, he was beaten around the head with a large, heavy, steel mess-kitchen soup ladle. 'Have you ever seen the size of an army soup ladle?' he asks. His head and face were covered in bumps and bruises. It was gratuitous brutality from Private Evans's mates. There was no attempt at interrogation.

There was no point. There was no evidence against him. Shortly after this incident, Bradley went on the run. 'I couldn't stay in Unity. I couldn't walk out the door without being stopped.'

For the next year he was hardly in the same house three days running. His mother's home in Unity Walk was raided – sometimes ten times a week in 1973, sometimes twice a night – and the raiding parties did lots of damage. As well as general destruction, individual soldiers often took pleasure in destroying personal items – photographs, statues, sacred pictures. And some regiments were notorious for petty theft; they specialised in stealing money for domestic bills left, as was the custom in those days, behind the clock on the mantelpiece. They even stole jeans off washing lines. There would not have been much left unscathed in Bradley's home by the end of 1973.

Destruction of property by raiding parties was so common that in the early seventies the St Vincent de Paul society in Belfast had a depot on the Antrim Road which contained furniture that could be given out to replace wardrobes, tables, chairs and similar articles wantonly destroyed in 'searches'. The whole process was soul-destroying for the women like Bradley's mother and new wife, who struggled to maintain a home in the midst of repeated army raids.

While on the run, Bradley always stayed in the third battalion area, but never in Unity Flats – it was too small and too difficult to escape from, and too obvious. It was women who organised safe houses for those on the run. 'You'd contact a woman and say, "We need beds for two or three guys", and she'd organise it. You'd stay a couple of nights, and move on.' By the time Bradley was on the run in November 1972, the IRA had rented flats outside republican districts where there would not be a heavy security-force presence. Favourite streets for renting flats in the third-battalion area were beside a police barracks three kilometres up the Antrim Road from Unity Flats. Sympathisers in middle-class districts also offered a bed for the night. 'I've stayed with teachers and businessmen. I've stayed in the houses of hospital consultants, dentists and business people, who mightn't be going to jail if I was found, but they'd be losing their business.'

Unable to move freely in Unity as company OC, he sometimes held meetings with the company staff in the New Lodge to plan 'ops', to receive intelligence reports, to liaise and coordinate with other companies in the third battalion. He also selected men for training in camps in the south. IRA men and sympathisers in the south organised the camps, supplying food, weaponry and equipment. 'The Southerners were brilliant. They had everything set up. The Free Staters [Bradley's name for the authorities in the Republic] knew the IRA was training in camps there. The Guards turned a blind eye. They gave you a "bye ball". They knew rightly. Anyway, they had to know because we were firing heavy weapons a lot of the time, hundreds of rounds.'

For a time, one of G company's members was Patrick Magee, later to be jailed for life for his part in the 1984 Brighton bomb attack on the Conservative party conference. Magee's people had emigrated to England. They returned to Belfast and lived in Unity

Walk where Magee's family was friendly with Bradley's. At an early stage in the Troubles, the Magee family moved back to England, but Patrick stayed behind to operate in the IRA. He 'ran about' with Gerry Bradley. Bradley says Magee fought hard to get into the IRA. He was suspect because of his English accent. Bradley pushed his case.

Magee was interned in 1974 and released on the same day as Bradley in 1976. He had nowhere permanent to live, so Bradley gave him a key to his house in Unity, though that would not have been an especially clever place for an IRA man to choose to stay. Bradley remembers Magee being an explosives officer from the very outset. 'He was based in the Markets making the "blowy stuff" for the whole [third] battalion for weeks on end.' Since the Markets district was in the process of slum clearance and had suffered from serious industrial decline, there were plenty of derelict premises and yards where Magee could perfect his expertise in 'a well-ventilated open space', according to the recommendation of the hospital consultant to avoid irritation of the skin.

Bradley too spent a lot of time in 1973 in the Markets. 'I was using "floats" there because the Brits were wiping out the Markets.' A 'float' was a 'floating weapon', one available in a hurry, not in a sealed dump. 'A woman could bring it quick and get it back in a hurry.' A float was used for opportunistic shooting at army patrols. 'You could take a couple of shots, hand over the weapon, run to a parked car and take off.' Bradley remembers one occasion, when 'there was nothing happening in the Markets and the Brits were having it easy', stealing a Mini, putting an Armalite in the boot, driving into the Markets, 'blattering away at the Brits with it and driving straight back to Unity. It came out of nowhere. The Brits had no idea what was happening.' There would have been immediate retribution in the Markets: cordons, searches, arrests. After a shooting in the Markets, no one would have thought the gunmen would be miles away in Unity Flats or the New Lodge.

But Bradley was very nearly caught on one of his forays into the Markets in 1973. He had been 'giving a hand on a float' and as he and another man, Freddie, came out of a 'call house' (a place where IRA men could meet before an operation or if there was a problem to sort out) and heard what he thought was the distinctive engine whine of an armoured car. The heavy military presence in the Markets meant a patrolling vehicle was always likely to appear. 'Inglis bakery was still in business in the Markets then and there was constant noise from its machinery. I says to Freddie, "Is that an armoured car engine?" "No," says he, "that's Inglis bakery working away."' Bradley turned into the next street and there was the 'pig', army slang for a one-ton Humber armoured personnel carrier, a ubiquitous vehicle on Belfast streets. He instantly turned back around the corner and dived into a house. Too late, he'd been recognised. The pig began circling two streets, its commander radioing for reinforcements that quickly arrived, cordoned off the streets where they knew Bradley and the other man were, and started house-to-house searches.

'Freddie dived into what they called in Belfast then a 'coal-hole' in the back yard of a house. Luckily, there had recently been a delivery, so he was able to bury himself under a pile of coal. I got into the house of a relative, Nell Moss, without the Brits spotting me. I ran upstairs to a bedroom, but it was bare except for a bed and a wee wardrobe. In those days people didn't have much in the way of possessions. I scrambled under the bed, and there was a full chamber pot; there was outside toilets in the Markets then. I got in behind it and lay tight against the wall. I pulled the sheet down as far as I could.'

Meanwhile out in the street about a dozen women, including Nell Moss, were praying silently, thereby confirming for the soldiers they were 'warm'. Were they praying for divine intervention to enable the men to escape? Was it so that the soldiers wouldn't shoot the IRA men? Was it to comfort themselves? Was it plain stupidity – drawing attention to the street?

'I was lying under the bed. A soldier started to come up the stairs. It was like in slow motion, like a Hitchcock movie. "Clomp, clomp, clomp" – his boots coming up the stairs. My heart was hammering. I could hardly breathe. I heard him opening the wee wardrobe. Then he lifted the sheet, saw the po and said, "Dirty bastards." He just clomped out again. I was shaking. I couldn't believe it. I just lay there until the women came up and said the Brits were gone. No idea how long that was. Seemed like hours, though it was probably about twenty minutes. The women came in shouting, "Where are you?" When I told them I'd been saved by the po, they roared laughing.' It was the nearest Bradley came in 1973 to being arrested.

Others were not so lucky. Soldiers on patrol knew who they were looking for and sometimes arresting them was not always on the agenda. While Ardoyne and the New Lodge, in the IRA's third battalion area, were a good deal bigger than Unity Flats, they were both compact districts nevertheless, each about two and a half square kilometres. In early 1973 there was another third battalion operating in those districts: the British army third battalion, the Parachute Regiment, who developed a reputation not only for gratuitous brutality but for shooting IRA men on sight. There were several controversial incidents when men at street corners or walking along a street were shot and killed. Others were wounded. Sometimes the victims were in the IRA, sometimes not. Some soldiers were trigger-happy. In January 1973 a soldier shot dead a seventy-six-year-old Protestant woman in Ardoyne, claiming he had seen 'a gunman'. The army apologised. Locals said the army had opened fire on four men at a street corner as the unfortunate woman walked round the corner.

Not all regiments were as frightful as the Paras. Bradley says that 'compared to the Marines or Paras, the Queen's regiment were "bums".' He is not even sure if they were the Queen's regiment or the Queen's Lancashire regiment, or what the difference is. He remembers sitting on a wall in Unity Flats with his friend 'Coke' when a patrol from one of these regiments came past. Recognising the two seated on the wall, the intelligence officer, a captain, stopped, swaggered over to them and said, 'If anyone shoots at my men, you, [pointing to Coke] are going to jail, and [pointing to

Bradley] we'll shoot you.' Next afternoon, as a foot patrol made its way through Unity to Clifton Street with the same captain among its number, Bradley opened up with a burst from an Armalite. The captain dropped his rifle and took to his heels. He was demoted to lieutenant and was afterwards known in Unity as 'Johnny-Two--Pips' because a lieutenant wears two pips on his epaulette to a captain's three.

Behind the relentless patrolling and searching, however, the army was concentrating on cultivating its informers inside the IRA in order to chop off the head of the organisation. They wanted to lift battalion and company OCs and, of course, brigade and battalion staff. 'I didn't know there was any strategy like that. I just thought they knew who was who. They certainly seemed to, because there were few innocent men in Long Kesh after 1972.'

No one, apart from the British, knows exactly when Eamon Molloy began working for them, but it was sometime in 1972. Molloy was from the Bone, home to a small, tough, tight-knit community beside Ardoyne. His background as a third battalion IRA operator was impeccable – except that when he was lifted in 1972 and taken to Castlereagh, unlike hundreds of other republicans he did not end up in Long Kesh but claimed he had escaped, which, if true, would have meant that he was the only man ever to do so. The IRA's Belfast Brigade bought the story. The truth was that Molloy had been turned. Soon, as more and more key men were lifted, Molloy graduated from third battalion staff to brigade staff, as Belfast quartermaster in 1973. That, in itself, was highly unusual and a measure of the esteem in which Molloy was held. Unusual because, Bradley says, 'None of the third batt, with the exception of Jim Brown, ever got to brigade staff because they thought we were sectarian, but it *was* one of our jobs to hit back at loyalist attacks. It was okay for first and second batt to talk, but places like Andersonstown only had the Brits to worry about. The loyalists were always having a go at us.'

As for Molloy, he was passing crucial information to the British and, using his position as quartermaster, he was giving away huge quantities of materiel, including his own dump in Ardoyne. Bradley says it was a battalion dump, 'a lot of big stuff'. Bradley still shakes his head in disbelief at what Molloy did. He says he was 'a very personable, likeable guy, with "no side" to him.' Molloy's information also led to heavy attrition in the third battalion as one battalion OC after another was arrested from safe houses or call houses. Martin Meehan, the main figure in Ardoyne was arrested in 1972 at a location probably named by Molloy, followed by two other battalion OCs. In July 1973 Molloy gave information that led to the arrest of the main figures in the Belfast Brigade, including the Belfast Brigade commander, Gerry Adams, and his operations officer, the formidable Brendan 'Darkie' Hughes. Shortly afterwards, soldiers arrested almost the whole third battalion staff at a meeting in Ardoyne, all on the word of Molloy.

It would be two years before the Belfast IRA tied together the common thread connecting these and a series of other arrests in safe houses. Unfortunately, most of those doing the tying together were in Long Kesh as a result of the common thread. One of them was Darkie Hughes, arrested three times, each time after escaping from custody and going into hiding, only for his hiding place to be given away by Molloy. Finally, sometime in spring 1975 the penny dropped. Eamon Molloy was taken in by the IRA's internal security people, tortured, interrogated and shot dead.

So embarrassed and shocked was the IRA's Belfast leadership by the vast amount of information about men and materiel Molloy had given away to the British, and by their own gullibility and incompetence in dealing with his informing, that they kept his activities and death at their hands a secret for twenty-four years. It wasn't until May 1999 that his body was given up to relatives as part of the peace process. That same year, in April 1999, an IRA source told the nationalist *Irish News* that 'about twenty-five to thirty top men were arrested on the information of Molloy.' That's an educated guess: only the British army knows the full extent of the information he supplied.

As more and more senior men were arrested in Belfast throughout 1973, Gerry Bradley found himself in autumn that year promoted from OC G company to OC third battalion at the age of nineteen, the youngest battalion commander in the IRA. It was Ivor Bell, Adams's successor as OC Belfast Brigade, a man also to fall victim to Molloy, who appointed Bradley. Bradley's father had trained Bell in the 1950s and Bell believed, correctly, that Bradley was a sound choice: loyal, zealous, leading from the front and impossible to turn, given his family history and unthinking commitment to the IRA. In fact, of course, in the last analysis, Bradley was appointed for the same reason that Molloy went unsuspected for so long. IRA leaders in Belfast could not bring themselves to imagine that someone from a republican district like the Bone would give away his mates or set them up for British soldiers to shoot. It just so happened that in Bradley's case they were correct, but they never checked him out any more than they did Molloy.

However sound a selection Bradley was for his commitment, reliability and loyalty to the IRA, he, like most IRA men, was first and foremost an operator, not an administrator. As OC third battalion, he had battalion staff: adjutant, quartermaster, EO, IO, TO, FO, whom he had to try to meet regularly. With the finance officer he had to fund the battalion, which meant planning robberies: banks and post offices mainly. 'One week we might do two or three, the next week nothing. We'd normally get about £2,000, which was okay – for 1973, remember.' With the quartermaster, he had to acquire and allocate weaponry, which meant constant bitching with the Belfast Brigade and the seven companies in the third battalion. With the explosives officer he had to organise supplies of 'mix' (homemade explosive), and detonators for bombs – and so on, and so on, through the various responsibilities of all the various staff.

He had seven companies to coordinate, as well as a new development to take into account: a Belfast Brigade squad, known for PR purposes as an 'active service unit' (ASU). To prevent companies in the battalion clashing in their operations, every company OC sent in a 'chock' (a written report) to Bradley each day, listing the operations proposed in the company area. The chocks all had to be into a shop in Clifton Street by 11.00am. Bradley would send a girl to collect them and then he would decide which operations to authorise and supply. He had to have regular meetings with the Belfast Brigade staff to ensure that the new brigade squad was not planning to operate somewhere one of the third-battalion companies was engaged.

It was all too much for Bradley. At nineteen, he did not have the experience to deal with this amount of paperwork and meetings. Temperamentally, he did not have the patience or inclination either.

'There was a lot of jealousy and back-stabbing. I suppose there is in any organisation. Other people wanted to be battalion OC. You got this constant begrudging, people running, complaining – politics, I suppose. I just wanted to get on with the biz. There were regular rows. I had company OCs who didn't want to do anything, but they wanted to be OC, full stop. I was on their case. I had one big row with brigade because I cancelled three ops in a battalion-size op because I didn't think the companies concerned were ready. Brigade said the ops should have gone ahead.

'We also moved the battalion staff up the Cavehill Road, out of the New Lodge and Ardoyne, where we could meet in a bit of peace. Maybe that was a mistake because you didn't know what was happening on the street. It distanced you from where the action was. You were relying on chocks. I was also remote from Bawnmore and the Short Strand. Didn't know what was going on there. I'm getting all this stuff coming in, but can I take decisions on it? What's not coming in?'

Bradley was much happier at the sharp end. He was such a prolific operator that his elevation to battalion OC actually meant a reduction in IRA operations in the third battalion area. After a couple of months, Bell brought Billy Kelly up from the Republic, where he had gone to escape the attentions of the North's security forces, to replace Bradley as third battalion OC. Bradley moved to become battalion Intelligence Officer towards the end of 1973. Kelly was in his thirties, highly experienced, having previously acted as third battalion OC in 1970, and was at the stage where he was not much use on operations, whereas Bradley, at nineteen and hyperactive, was indispensable.

While the helter-skelter of violence careered in full spate around Belfast's streets, the British government had been working hard to create a political settlement. Most importantly, the British had accepted that the North's nationalist community must play a full role in the state. For the first time since 1921, they had also acknowledged the legitimate interest of the Irish government in the affairs of the North: northern secretary Willie Whitelaw called it 'the Irish dimension'. In June 1973, there had been elections to a new Northern Ireland assembly whose parties were to negotiate a new political arrangement for the North acceptable to the British and Irish governments. Unfortunately, such a new arrangement would not be acceptable either to the majority of unionists or to the republican movement, who saw the concessions the British had made only as vindication of their military campaign.

In December 1973, at the British Civil Service college at Sunningdale in Berkshire, the two main political parties, the Ulster Unionists (UUP) and the Social Democratic and Labour Party (SDLP), reached agreement on a power-sharing executive to administer Northern Ireland, with seats in the executive distributed proportionately between unionists and nationalists. To the astonishment of many nationalists, and the horror of many unionists, Brian Faulkner, the UUP leader and last prime minister of Northern Ireland, agreed to act as chief executive alongside the leader of the nationalist SDLP Gerry Fitt, who would be deputy chief executive.

Like everyone else in the IRA, Gerry Bradley couldn't care less about these developments. He regarded the political process as irrelevant, a ploy by the British to allow them to continue to govern the North. Republicans couldn't believe there was any chance of equality for nationalists as long as Britain was involved in Ireland. That view was one of their basic tenets. 'Sunningdale was never going to get off the ground because we didn't want it to, wouldn't allow it. Guys like Billy McKee [one of the founders of the Provisional IRA and first Belfast Brigade commander] or Seamus Twomey [chief of staff for most of 1973] or Ivor Bell wouldn't accept anything less than a British withdrawal or a declaration of intent to do so. The Brits kept on about a ceasefire, but I saw that anxiety as a sign of weakness from them. I didn't want a political settlement. I wanted a withdrawal. I hadn't a political thought in my head. If the IRA told me to shoot somebody, I did, because the IRA was right.'

However, while the IRA leadership was vehemently opposed to the political developments, they were not oblivious to what was going on. They adamantly rejected the creation of Sunningdale's political structures, not only because there was no mention of a British withdrawal, but mainly because republicans had not been involved in devising those structures. Furthermore, they believed the rationale behind Sunningdale was to exclude and isolate republicans. The IRA leaders determined to destroy Sunningdale.

Ironically, the majority of unionists also took a position of resolute opposition to Sunningdale, but, of course, for reasons diametrically opposed to those of republicans. For them, the involvement of the Irish government in negotiations, leading to compulsory power-sharing with nationalists and the proposal for a Council of Ireland, were a 'sell-out', an abject surrender to the IRA, a reward for violence. The loudest voice in objection to the deal was that of Ian Paisley, who, twenty-five years later, would enter into a similar arrangement with the former chief of staff of the IRA, Martin McGuinness.

'Sunningdale was to come into operation in January 1974. Around the time of the agreement in December, or maybe November, when the outline of the power-sharing deal had been revealed – I can't remember precisely – me and another third battalion operator, Mickey P from the New Lodge, were selected to shoot Brian Faulkner.'

Had they succeeded, there is no doubt there would have been no executive, such was the unionist opposition to the whole concept and such would have been the cataclysmic repercussions throughout the North.

A British Ministry of Defence document from November 1973 shows that British military intelligence had already considered the possibility of an attack on Faulkner. Marked 'Secret UK Eyes', the document is entitled 'Protestant Extremism – The Threat'. Under the heading 'Circumstances likely to produce extensive Protestant terrorism' the memo to the General Officer Commanding from a staff colonel says:

> There are a number of possible events which could promote a significant change in the political and security situation. One of these, which could be almost catastrophic in its consequences would be the assassination of Brian Faulkner.

The IRA had information that Faulkner was speaking at an Orange hall near Newcastle, County Down. Bradley thinks – and this is not altogether far-fetched – it might have come from disaffected unionists opposed to Faulkner's intention to share power with nationalists. Faulkner would have two police bodyguards.

'The night Faulkner was to make that speech, me and Mickey met with Jim Brown, Belfast Brigade adjutant, in a flat in

Stranmillis.' Stranmillis is a quiet, middle-class district in south Belfast, where no one would expect an IRA squad to gather. Stranmillis also had the advantage on being near the route out of Belfast to Newcastle.

'Jim Brown told us the plan was to kill Faulkner and we were to do it. He gave us sub-machine guns. We were to be picked up from the flat in Stranmillis by IRA men from south Down – "countrymen".'

The plan was simple, ruthless and hair-raising. 'We were going to be taken somewhere in the County Down countryside. Once there, we would transfer to a car which had its rear window removed. As Faulkner was driven from the meeting with two RUC bodyguards, the man driving me and Mickey, a countryman with local knowledge, would overtake the police car carrying Faulkner and we would "sub" him out the back window, give him the message.' From Bradley's description, the assassination was probably planned to take place on a long, straight section of road, past the Seaforde estate north of the loyalist village of Clough. 'The Belfast Brigade knew their men. Me and Mickey would have done it. I wanted to do it.'

The plan to kill Faulkner must have come from the very top of the IRA because of its huge political and security consequences. Faulkner was a hate figure in the nationalist community. He somewhat redeemed himself in 1974 by participating in the power-sharing executive and facing down loyalist extremists, as well as Paisley and his supporters, but his record, stretching back twenty years before 1973, was of unremitting hostility to nationalism, tinged with a strong dose of anti-Catholic bigotry, regularly displayed on platforms at Orange fields over the years. Of course, the IRA correctly blamed him as the man who had persuaded the British, against their better judgement and military advice, to introduce internment in 1971 and who had personally endorsed the arrest of men who had never been involved in violence, including civil rights agitators and members of a Trotskyist student group, the People's Democracy. His death would have been greeted with universal celebration in republican districts. It would have stopped Sunningdale in its tracks. It would also have caused widespread civil disturbance across the North and the deaths of many innocent Catholics.

'I had a bad feeling about the operation from the word go, but I was still ready to do it. All I knew was the third batt area. I didn't know south or east Belfast, never mind the Newcastle area. I asked what would happen if we had to dump the car, and the answer was, "Every man in the Belfast Brigade will be looking for youse." I knew then it was a one-way ticket. We were going to be dead or in jail.' How were men from the Belfast Brigade, most of whom knew nothing about County Down and weren't even aware of the night's operation against Faulkner, supposed to be looking for him and Mickey in the back of beyond?

As they waited with increasing trepidation for the 'off', word came that the operation was cancelled. Faulkner wasn't speaking at the meeting, or arrangements with the local IRA unit had broken down – Bradley can't remember why. He and Mickey were stood down. Perhaps the operation had been compromised. Who knew about it? Would Molloy, brigade quartermaster, have known that sub-machine guns were being supplied and for what purpose? Was the operation discussed at a brigade staff meeting?

Whether or not that particular operation was compromised, the Belfast IRA certainly knew that information was passing to the British at an alarming rate. The big battalions, which had grown to hundreds of volunteers in 1972, were bound to be leaky. Even if there had not been many informers, men drank and talked and gossiped. Something had to be done to stem the flow.

Towards the end of Bradley's time as battalion OC in 1973, the Belfast adjutant, Jim Brown, arranged to meet him in a call house in Willowbank Gardens, one of the third battalion's favourite streets beside the RUC barracks on the Antrim Road, a respectable address outside hard-line republican districts. There, Brown told Bradley it had been decided to restructure the whole army. The old battalions were going. There were going to be 'squads'. Publicly they would be known as 'active service units' or ASUs. There already was one operating across the Belfast Brigade for some time, but now a number were going to be established independently of each battalion area. He told Bradley to get the men in each company in the battalion to write out a 'chock', listing all the ops they'd been on – essentially a CV. That way, brigade would be able to select the best men for the squads. Bradley thought it was madness to have documents like that floating around. Although the chocks wouldn't be signed, it would be obvious who the men were in each case. Little did he know he need not have worried because Eamon Molloy was telling British intelligence everything of importance the brigade was up to anyway.

'Once selected for a squad, a man was brought away from the company. Some were told to say they'd jacked it in: it was too risky, or some such excuse.' The squads were small – four to six men, up to ten – better and tighter organised than the big companies. They wouldn't know members of other squads. They could co-opt individuals for specific purposes, but the co-opted ones wouldn't know the members of a squad, maybe only one. They got better training and equipment. They began to have their own weapons and dumps. They operated across battalion boundaries. 'Squads were the right idea. You could have maybe ten in a squad, all from different areas of Belfast. It was hard for the Brits to tie the men together. They didn't socialise together, meet for a drink or anything. They could move you from one squad to another for different ops.'

There was another advantage from the IRA leadership's viewpoint. The squads reduced the status of battalion and company commanders, and thereby reduced the autonomy of battalions, which enabled Belfast Brigade to exert tighter control over operations and supersede local control. Company commanders did not always know the squads operating in their districts. In time, there would be no need for company commanders and battalion commanders. Brigade authorised the operations of the squads. It was a good idea, but no one knew then that brigade itself was compromised.

Bradley was also compromised. One morning in January 1974, he was at a call house on the Limestone Road in north Belfast with the new third battalion OC, Billy Kelly, when another IRA man, called Green, came to the house. Green had been released from Castlereagh Holding Centre the night before, after forty-eight hours' detention. He announced that there was a guy down in the Rotterdam bar in the Docks pretending to be an IRA man and demanding money. Bradley decided to go immediately to deal with him, despite Billy Kelly telling him to check it out, to wait, there was no hurry, it wasn't even eleven o'clock in the morning. Bradley, headstrong as ever, headed off in a car to the Rotterdam bar.

He walked into the bar. There was no one there. British soldiers came in instantly and arrested him. Green had set him up. His long run was over. For a few hours in North Queen Street joint RUC/army barracks, he managed to stick convincingly to his cover story that he was not Gerry Bradley but a local teacher with a different name. He had ID, was dressed for the part, with shirt and tie, and was carrying a briefcase. However, inevitably the police would check out his ID and find that the real teacher was in class a short distance away. In the end, to save disruption of the school and the embarrassment and probable arrest of the real teacher he was impersonating, Bradley finally admitted who he was. To his surprise, the police cheered and shouted to colleagues outside the room, who also cheered. At last they had got Bradley.

He was served with a detention order alleging that, 'at various times he held the ranks of Officer Commanding Fianna,

Operations Officer, Finance Officer, Quartermaster and Officer Commanding in the Provisional IRA at company and battalion level.' It was a fair summary of his busy previous three years, except for the role of Finance Officer: that was Nan Saunders, mother of Jim Saunders, a member of F company shot dead by British soldiers in the Bone in February 1971.

6

WAR AS A WAY OF LIFE

'By the end of 1976, it was known that there were regular
beatings in the H-blocks, that you could be isolated
in your cell and kept practically in solitary
confinement or in a punishment cell.
Sentences were enormous. There was no prospect of escape from the
H-blocks. There was no sign of an end to the conflict on the outside.
What would a man do if sentenced? Go on the blanket, endure the
beatings and punishments for years on end, or conform and accept
being labelled a criminal?'

Bradley's longer period of internment from 1974-75 was very different from the first period, which lasted for five months in 1972. After his arrest in 1972, he was taken straight from Girdwood barracks to the *Maidstone* prison ship, where he had come under the wing of Kevin Hannaway. Bradley was fully integrated into the Provisional ranks.

His experience when he had arrived in Long Kesh in January 1974 was in complete contrast. He had spent forty-eight hours in Castlereagh, the maximum time allowed in those days. The RUC in Castlereagh had not arrested him on any specific charge, and were just glad to have him in indefinite custody, like so many other IRA men. He had been processed and consigned to Long Kesh.

Like everyone else arriving in Long Kesh after being in Castlereagh, Bradley was routinely debriefed about his time there. Being completely innocent of passing any information to the police, Bradley naively gave a full account to the camp bosses of what had happened. Unfortunately, he had made the tactical error of saying to the police in Castlereagh that he had once been in the IRA, but had left it. Admitting membership of the IRA, or indeed answering any RUC questions at all, was forbidden by army rules. His debriefers seized on this minor, and to Bradley, inconsequential, point. After all, he had lied to the police rather than told them anything of consequence. Bradley was extremely annoyed, and, depressed with the shock of being captured, especially the way he had walked into it, he was in no mood to put up with any nonsense from the camp bosses. Bradley was furious with them and a row ensued in which he squared up to the senior man debriefing him.

In those first days in Long Kesh, he did not appreciate how important the camp bosses considered themselves to be, nor how important it was for him to bend the knee to them. In the pressure-cooker atmosphere of Long Kesh, it was vital to give such people their place if you wanted an easy time. Instead, Bradley confronted the top men. In this initial confrontation, Bradley let fly verbally at them: 'What do youse know about operations? How many operations have you ever done?' He called two brothers from west Belfast, important in the camp hierarchy, 'fat, yellow bastards'.

As a result, despite references being sent into the jail from his third battalion colleagues in north Belfast and from the Belfast Brigade Intelligence Officer to confirm that Bradley had given no information to the police, that the same safe houses were being used and the same dumps remained secure, Bradley was not accepted into the ranks in Long Kesh. The senior men in the camp refused to clear him, though they knew perfectly well he had given no information. Instead, he was suspended from the IRA. Bradley was frustrated and infuriated, but powerless to do anything to redress his grievance against people he considered stupid and hidebound. It was a very unhappy time for Bradley.

His refusal to be subservient to the powers that be in the camp continued to cause problems for him after his release, because the men he had confronted on his internment in 1974 had been released before him and they blocked his return to active service.

Internment was at its most wretched in 1974 and 1975. The numbers interned had been growing steadily since Operation Motorman in 1972. Hundreds of men were crushed into the Nissen huts. The fabric of Long Kesh began to fall apart under the strain. Nothing worked. The corrugated-iron huts were damp and freezing most of the time, but like ovens on sunny days. Food was terrible, usually served on trays covered in tinfoil and cold when it arrived. Often the warders maliciously ruined food parcels sent in by relatives. Lighting, when it worked, was dim. Men made their own makeshift lamps – 'Long Kesh candles', with butter in tobacco tins for fuel and shoelaces for wicks. Then there was the boredom.

Worst of all, according to Bradley, were the mind games the authorities played. 'Guys would get out for no reason. People would sit and wonder why. Then nobody in the cage would get out for a couple of months. Why? Parcels would be stopped. Why? Parole would be given to some at Christmas, not others. Why? Everybody wandered about, asking, "Any *scéal*? [news]". What was happening? How long would it last?'

Indeterminate internment causes serious psychological problems. At least with a sentence, men knew when they were supposed to be free and counted the days. With internment, no one knew. 'A lot of guys had had a hard time in Girdwood or Palace barracks. They couldn't get their heads round what was happening to them. Some guys refused visits. Sometimes the IRA ordered people to refuse visits because the screws had changed some rule, like having to take your shoes off. Marriages broke up. Some guys never recovered from the mind games.

'Sometimes the Brit soldiers would raid a cage. They'd come in at 4.00 or 5.00 in the morning and beat you, wreck your stuff. Guys would retaliate. The Brits had this rule that when they came in, you were supposed to lie dead flat on your bed, with your arms by your sides, and face the ceiling, look straight at it. The IRA told men not to comply. Alex Maskey [now Sinn Féin's Chief Whip in Stormont] got a massive beating with batons one time for refusing to comply. Maskey just happened to be in the first bunk the Brits came to when they entered.

'One guy, Tommy Gorman, led a group of young IRA men,

known as "Gorman's Gorillas", in his hut. They never even attempted to follow the rules about lying flat. As soon as the Brits came in, Gorman's lot all went straight at them. There was mayhem. Tommy Gorman was beaten unconscious repeatedly.'

Eventually, the resentment exploded in October 1974. There had been a constant war of attrition between the governor, Robert Truesdale, and IRA officers about a long list of grievances: raids, searches, destruction of possessions, quality of food, recreation, frequency and length of visits and so on. 'Harry Fitz, the camp OC, came back one day from dealing with the governor and said, "Truesdale says the honeymoon is over." We took that to mean things were going to get even worse. The decision was taken to burn the camp. The IRA camp staff had threatened that before, but now they decided enough was enough.

'It was one of the best days of my life. There were a couple of guys assigned to burn each hut. Me and another guy, Seamus, from Strabane, burnt our hut. I think I was in Cage 4 by then. Men burst open the gates of each cage, broke open the solitary cells, burnt the kitchens: burnt everything. We couldn't get to the sentenced men's end to join up, but they were wrecking and burning things too. It was a brilliant feeling, but we knew we were in for it.

'Next day I never saw as many British troops in all my life. Hundreds of them in full riot gear: batons, shields, steel helmets, visors, rubber bullet guns. Hundreds and hundreds of them, in marching order. We got ready with bedposts, bits of wood, chisels, the odd spike – homemade stuff. We were outnumbered about two to one.

There was hand-to-hand fighting at the sentenced end. Some guys were seriously battered. Guys were taken to hospital. A lot of Brits got injured too.

'The Brits fired rubber bullets at point-blank range. John Joe McGirl [former IRA chief of staff and Sinn Féin TD for Sligo–Leitrim in 1957, aged 53 in 1974] was hit in the face by a rubber bullet and had a gigantic bruise. His face was swollen like three snooker balls. McGirl had been ready to make a speech at Milltown cemetery when he was arrested. They found his speech curled up in his ear and it was threatening all kinds of serious IRA action. So he was interned.

'The Brits fired gas and dropped gas from a helicopter. They say it was CR gas, about ten times stronger than CS; some say it was CN gas – even worse – but the Brits deny it all.

'Eventually, the Brit CO called on the IRA camp OC to parley. After that the IRA dropped their weapons. The Brits kept us spread-eagled, leaning up against the wire for about five hours. It was cutting the hands off us. Some guys fell down. Eventually one guy, Maguire, turned round and said to the Brits guarding him, and I know this is ridiculous, "You're only doing this because we're Catholics." Like, it wasn't anything to do with wrecking the place? The Brits attacked him and a big guy, Tommy Reilly, from Bally-murphy, turned round and said, "Leave the wee lad alone." One soldier said to Reilly, "You shut up." Reilly faced him. Then every-body began to stand up and turn round. It was a stand-off. It was tense. It looked like it was all going to start again.

'Then the Brits picked up our homemade weapons where they were lying on the ground and they left us. We were a few days in the open, nearly a week – no shelter, freezing and starving. They gave us milk in cartons. After you drank the milk, they put soup in the carton; but the Brits had put maggots in the soup and it was cold. Some guys took it anyway.'

A shared experience, like the burning of Long Kesh and the events surrounding it, produced a sense of solidarity and a feeling of camaraderie among the inmates. There were other, happier memories, which equally served to enhance camaraderie. For example, the internees developed what Bradley calls 'spectacular drill'.

'Sentenced prisoners had been doing a bit of drilling, but it wasn't until Martin Meehan became OC on the internees' side that real drilling came in. Meehan was interned immediately after he had served his sentence. He made everyone drill. It was a guy called Hugh Carson who organised it; his brother, Billy, got shot dead in Manor Street in 1979.

'At the start it was hopeless – guys crashing into each other. The Brits came and laughed, shouted out wrong orders, had guys turning every way, made eejits of us. After three months, it was perfection. Off-duty Brits came to watch. There was no laughing then. They came to admire. It was brilliant. It put the fear of God into the Brits, seeing hundreds of IRA marching, wheeling, turning on a sixpence. The drilling kept morale up. Kept people fit.'

However, there was a dark side to internment as well, which Bradley experienced to a minor degree. The IRA camp staff wielded absolute power and, as Bradley often points out, the people who were hardest on IRA men were the IRA. Inside the camp, or in later years in prison, after internment had ended, men on the receiving end of petty injustices from IRA camp bosses had no one to turn to. There were complaint mechanisms and procedures in the IRA, but the main injunction was to 'speak from within', that is to say, to keep your complaints within the IRA structures. The worst crime of all was to make your objections known outside the movement, to let the side down. 'Speak from within' also meant that you had to be in the IRA to speak about it. No one listened to any strictures or complaints from anyone not in the IRA, and that included people in Sinn Féin.

In the early days of internment and right up to about 1974, men who had broken under interrogation in Palace barracks or Girdwood were ostracised when they arrived in Long Kesh. No one spoke to them. They had to eat separately in some cages. In some cages they were badly beaten. One man lost an inch off his leg he was so badly beaten. Bradley says: 'These were all just internees. These guys being treated like shit were only seventeen and eighteen sometimes. They'd never been away from home. They'd been in a barracks once in their lives. Then the IRA was beating their own after they'd come through somewhere like Palace barracks, which was a torture chamber. It was stopped by the IRA outside. It was bad publicity. It didn't make sense to outsiders. Here we were, complaining about the Brits torturing people, and the IRA was beating its own people.'

Gerry Bradley emerged from Long Kesh in November 1975 to a changed world. The nature and intensity of the violence had altered fundamentally since he had been interned in 1974. On the face of it, the Troubles might have looked as though they were continuing unabated: 1976 would be the second bloodiest year of the Troubles after 1972, with 307 dead. It could also be argued that the considerable drop in casualties, from 304 people killed in 1974 to 206 in 1975, was only a dip, largely because of a twelve-month IRA ceasefire from March 1975. However, annual casualty numbers after 1976 fell substantially: down to 116 dead in 1977 and 88 in 1978.

This decline was the most obvious consequence of the less intense conflict on the streets of Belfast and Derry. The conflict had entered another phase. Gone were the days of daily gun battles and bombings and mass inter-communal strife, when dozens of houses were damaged or burnt. Measures had been introduced to keep bombers away from prestige targets in the centre of Belfast, which was now enclosed by steel palisade fences two and a half metres high, with gates manned by searchers during the day – a so-called 'ring of steel'. This security system did terrible damage to commercial life and meant Belfast was a ghost town after six in the evening, but, combined with regular vehicle check-points on the routes into the city from republican districts, the 'ring of steel' for the most part kept car bombs out of the centre of Belfast. Similar measures followed to protect the centres of most towns of any size across the North.

It is now clear that by 1976 both the British government and the IRA leadership were in the process of changing their strategies, so that both sides could settle in for a protracted struggle. On the IRA side, a crucial change was the establishment of Northern Command in 1976. That decision meant that the armed struggle was being directed by a small group of northerners around Gerry Adams, a group that would take control of the whole republican movement in the 1980s and was to remain substantially the same until the IRA stood down in 2005. They had supplanted the southern leadership of the campaign by arguing that the military decisions were best taken by the people engaged in the conflict.

The real reason, however, was that Adams and the group around him were furious at the ceasefire Ruairi Ó Brádaigh, Daithí Ó Conaill and the southern leadership had agreed in 1975. The northerners believed the ceasefire had seriously weakened the IRA and the republican negotiating position and had produced no political gains whatsoever. The northerners also strongly disagreed with the policy document called *Éire Nua* adopted by the southerners. It advocated a sort of federal arrangement with a nine-county Ulster, but, as far as the northerners were concerned, it meant unionists would discriminate against nationalists in a nine-county arena instead of in a six-county one.

The group Adams led had spent a long time in Long Kesh thinking out their strategy. They had resolved that the republican movement must develop a strong political wing, connect with people in the districts where they had most support and, in effect, establish an alternative administration to the British one, taking control of policing, justice and running day-to-day life in those areas. The role of the movement's political wing, Sinn Féin, would be greatly enhanced, though still under the control of the IRA. It was the very beginnings of what came to be known in republican circles as the 'civil administration'.

On the military side, instead of the emphasis on 'one last push', the northerners successfully argued for a strategic decision go for a 'long war'. Hopelessly optimistic slogans like '1973 the year of victory' were jettisoned, though it was not so easy to get rid of the mindset that produced them. There would be no glorious final victory. Gone were the days when IRA leaders thought that if they kept up the shooting and bombing relentlessly on a daily basis, the British would throw in the towel and leave. The IRA accepted that the British would not be driven into the sea at the end of a successful military campaign. The struggle instead would be a slogging match, ending in negotiations, and IRA members had to be prepared psychologically for all that. The aim now became to show that there would never be stability in the North as long as the British remained, that the IRA could keep at it endlessly and could not be beaten.

To some extent, that strategic objective succeeded quite quickly. In 1978 extracts from an intelligence report *Northern Ireland: Future Terrorist Trends*, by the then Brigadier JM Glover, head of the Defence Intelligence Staff in Britain, were leaked and printed in *Republican News*, the IRA's house journal. The report concluded among other things that, 'The Provisionals' campaign of violence is likely to continue while the British remain in Northern Ireland.' Glover also predicted that, 'There is no prospect in the next five years of any political change which will remove the *raison d'être* of the Provisional IRA.'

In the *New Statesman* in 1978, journalist Duncan Campbell wrote this:

> Prepared by the most senior army officer on the Defence Intelligence Staff, Brigadier J. M. Glover, the report was written last November, and subsequently fell into the hands of the IRA. It was circulated to army commands in December after clearance and approval at the highest level. Glover himself, now promoted to Major-General, recently became Commander of Land Forces in Northern Ireland – a clear indication that his report must broadly represent the view of Northern Ireland held inside the Ministry of Defence.
>
> The report admits that the Provisionals are essentially a working class organisation, based in the ghetto areas of the city and in the poorer rural areas ... The terrorists' abilities, their professionalism, and their expertise are all on the increase, the army believe.
>
> The Provisional IRA (PIRA) has the dedication and the sinews of war to raise violence intermittently to at least the level of early 1978, certainly for the foreseeable future ... Our evidence of the rank and file terrorists does not support the view that they are merely mindless hooligans drawn from the unemployed and unemployable. PIRA now trains and uses its members with some care. The Active Service Units (ASUs) are for the

most part manned by terrorists tempered by up to ten years of operational experience...

The leaking of this document may have left the army dismayed and the IRA delighted. But its real significance for the future of the province lies with the wider public from whom it was intended that such honest thinking should be kept away. The military head of the Defence Intelligence Staff says here that the present war in Ireland cannot be won. The IRA will continue, for the foreseeable future, to wage continuous attrition against the British presence. ... Politicians may speak of 'overcoming the gunmen and terrorists', but the army knows it cannot be done.

Though it was politically impossible to admit it publicly, British politicians had taken on board the thinking behind this report and before 1976 had prepared a longterm plan to deal with a continuing IRA campaign. Their main political initiative, the Sunningdale Agreement, had failed in 1974 and after one last effort to establish some basis of power-sharing in 1976 the British gave up attempting political progress and opted instead to manage the conflict, settling for the notion of 'an acceptable level of violence'.

Their plan can be summed up under two headings: 'criminalisation' and 'Ulsterisation'. Under the first heading, special category status would be abolished for IRA, UVF and UDA prisoners alike. Internment would be ended and anyone convicted would be treated like an ordinary prisoner and housed in a newly built high-security jail called the Maze, beside the old Long Kesh internment camp. The new jail would remove the romantic concept of

Above: The funeral of Gerry Bradley's uncle, Frank Duffy, a prominent Republican whose body was flown to Belfast after his death in Cuba in the 1960s. Gerry Bradley's father is circled (top) and Gerry Adams's father (bottom right).

Below: Gerry Bradley (left) and 'Blue' Kelly in the late 1970s.

Above: 1970s Belfast riot. As a teenager Gerry Bradley 'loved rioting'.
Teenage boys often stoned soldiers for hours at a time, risking injury or
death from rubber and later plastic bullets.

Below: Soldiers were safest surrounded by local kids. They patrolled as schools
closed and encouraged kids to play with military equipment.

Above: 1970s training camp. In the modern IRA women were equal members of squads, playing a full role in shooting and bombing operations.

Right: A trio of youths in the Divis area prepare to attack the army with petrol bombs after the death of Bobby Sands on hunger strike, May 1981.

THE ROYAL ULSTER CONSTABULARY

Headquarters

Brooklyn Knock Road Belfast Northern Ireland BT5 6LE

Telephone Belfast 650222 Telex 74482

Messrs Donnelly & Wall
Solicitors
Pearl Assurance House
2 Donegall Square East
BELFAST

Please reply to the Chief Constable

Your reference

Our reference

Date 28 August 1974

Dear Sirs

RE: GERALD BRADLEY - DETAINEE AT MAZE PRISON

I refer to your letter of 21 August 1974, which I have now had an opportunity of discussing with the Crown Solicitor who advises me to reply to your request for Further and Better Particulars of the allegations as follows:

Charge 1
(a)   It will be alleged that at various times your client has held the ranks of Officer Commanding Fianna, Operations Officer, Finance Officer, Quartermaster and Officer Commanding in the Provisional IRA at Company and Battalion level.

(b)   It is regretted that no further information can be given without the risk of endangering the safety of others.

Charge 2 6.18pm

Charge 3
(a)   11.11am

(b)   Presumably delayed action device.

Charge 4 0208pm

Charge 5 2006.

Charge 6 1720.

Above and opposite: Document committing Gerry Bradley to detention (internment).
The allegations against Bradley are detailed including the various IRA ranks he was
believed to have held. Other charges are not presented in detail in case he might deduce
how the security forces came to know of the incidents. Only times are given.

NORTHERN IRELAND (EMERGENCY PROVISIONS) ACT 1973

DETENTION OF TERRORISTS

D E T E N T I O N   O R D E R

Whereas I am satisfied that the person specified below has been concerned in -

~~the commission of an act of terrorism~~

~~the attempted commission of an act of terrorism~~

the direction, organisation/training of persons for the purpose of terrorism
Ground 1 proved.

-    and that his detention is necessary for the protection of the public:

NOW therefore I, a Commissioner appointed under the Northern Ireland (Emergency
Provisions) Act 1973, hereby order, in pursuance of Paragraphs 12 and 24 of
Schedule 1 of that Act, the detention of

GERALD BRADLEY

Dated this   17th day of September 1974

                                                    N G A Gosling
                                                    COMMISSIONER

To the Secretary of State, Stormont Castle, Belfast
    the Governor or person in charge of HM Prison, Maze
    the said

R Bt 45370 1 (m) 5/74 TP

Long Kesh Prison 1975. (l to r) Oliver Kelly, Billy Kelly, Gerry 'Whitey' Bradley and Terry McIvor shortly before their release.

Gerry Bradley's discharge papers, signed by Northern Secretary Merlyn Rees, releasing him from internment. Internment ended in December 1975 and a new prison regime began in 1976 in the infamous H-blocks.

NORTHERN IRELAND (EMERGENCY PROVISIONS) (AMENDMENT) ACT 1975

DIRECTION FOR DISCHARGE OF A PERSON DETAINED UNDER A DETENTION ORDER

THE SECRETARY OF STATE in pursuance of Paragraph 10(2)(a) of Schedule 1 of the Northern Ireland (Emergency Provisions) (Amendment) Act 1975 hereby directs that Gerald BRADLEY
                        8H Unity Walk
                        Belfast

a person detained under a detention order dated the   17th   day of   September 1974   be discharged from that order and be released unless he is in custody for some other cause.

Dated this   7th day of November 1975

ONE OF HER MAJESTY'S PRINCIPAL SECRETARIES OF STATE

To the Governor or other officer in charge of HM Prison ....Maze...........
and to the said .....Gerald BRADLEY..........

Above: Queen Street, Belfast 1977. IRA bombs had a devastating
effect on trade and commerce, chasing investors and making Belfast
a ghost town after 6.00 pm.

Below: The day after the night before. The results of a major Belfast riot, with thousands
of pounds worth of burnt-out vehicles littering the road, and the road surface melted.
Riots like these effectively made the district a no-go area for British troops.

Gerry Bradley today.

Unity Flats, showing the gable end facing Peter's Hill where loyalist mobs mounted their attacks on the flats in August 1969.

'prisoners of war' held in Nissen huts in World War II conditions, reminiscent of films like *The Great Escape*.

Secondly, 'Ulsterisation': the locally recruited militia, the overwhelmingly unionist Ulster Defence Regiment (UDR), would be increased in numbers and its role greatly enhanced, particularly in rural districts. The RUC would also be given upgraded weaponry, more heavily armoured Land Rovers, increased numbers and specialist units. Where possible they would take the lead role, reducing the British army's commitment.

There were several reasons for these changes. Expense was one. For example, having a sergeant in the Royal Artillery killed by a blast bomb in Belfast was not good economics when the man had been trained in the deployment of battlefield nuclear weapons in West Germany at a cost of £45,000 in 1975 values. Rotating all kinds of regiments, rather than deploying only infantry, meant that such highly trained specialists were exposed to the lottery of foot patrols on the streets of Northern Ireland.

In addition, keeping large numbers of regular troops in the North stretched the British army and deflected them from their main role as a NATO force facing the Red Army in West Germany and maintaining appropriate readiness for that role. Third, large numbers of British troops in the North helped confirm the IRA version of the Troubles, namely that it was a colonial war, with Britain holding on to part of Ireland against the will of the people; far better for the British case to have as many locals as possible dealing with the IRA. Thus, from the mid-seventies, the RUC and UDR were beefed up and moved as much as possible into the 'front line'. Of course, the result was more casualties for these locally recruited forces, but neither the army top brass nor British politicians would shed any tears about that since it was much preferable to having British 'squaddies' killed.

Finally, it would be necessary for the judiciary in the North to play a role by accepting evidence in non-jury courts that would not be countenanced anywhere else in the UK or Ireland. Judges went through the legal charade of 'warning themselves' that they were dealing with evidence a jury might reject. In most cases, they then went on to convict the accused even though in many, many instances it was solely on the basis of an unsigned 'confession'. The overwhelmingly unionist judiciary readily complied and, disgracefully, courts regularly handed down enormous sentences on the basis of such 'confessions'.

Even if men were not convicted, it was the norm for IRA suspects to be remanded in custody because they automatically jumped bail and headed for the safety of the Irish Republic. Scores of attempts by the British to have IRA suspects extradited failed. It was not until 1988 that an extradition act came into force and the first men were extradited north. For men remanded in custody in the North a two-year delay before they came to trial was not unusual. The court service pleaded pressure of work with the huge number of defendants. Republicans and civil liberty groups complained it was 'internment by remand', simply another ploy for taking IRA suspects off the streets.

The implementation of these British plans of 'Ulsterisation' and 'criminalisation' was to alter the nature of the republican struggle in ways the British officials who devised the policies could not have foreseen. The years 1976-81 marked a turning point, when the front line of struggle gradually moved from armed confrontations with the British army and car-bomb explosions in towns to the prisons, where IRA prisoners decided to mount a direct challenge to one of the British government's main lines of policy: criminalisation.

In the long tradition of republican prisoners, stretching back into the nineteenth century, the IRA prisoners sentenced after the new legislation, in 1976, rejected the attempt to brand them criminals. A truly titanic clash of wills between Margaret Thatcher's Conservative government and the IRA prisoners culminated in the hunger strikes of 1981, the deaths of ten republicans and the emergence of an enormously enhanced politicised republican movement that would ultimately capture the votes of the majority of northern nationalists.

Gerry Bradley was aware of some of the British policy changes, especially the changes to the penal regime. The spectre of 'the blocks' hung over all IRA men. These were the 'H-blocks' in the new prison, so-called because of their shape, with four wings of cells along each arm of the H and a central control area, called the 'circle', in the crossbar of the H. As soon as the new prison regime began in March 1976, IRA men refused to be treated as criminals: they wore blankets instead of prison garb and refused to do work.

That resistance, of course, meant they got no privileges and no remission.

It was a while before any information about conditions in the new prison leaked out. The first men convicted under the new regime were denied visits because they would not wear prison clothes, and they were not allowed to write letters because they were all being punished for refusal to conform, so for several months no one knew what was happening to them. By the end of 1976, however, it was known that there were regular beatings in the H-blocks, that you could be isolated in your cell and kept practically in solitary confinement or in a punishment cell. Sentences were enormous. There was no prospect of escape from the H-blocks. There was no sign of an end to the conflict on the outside. What would a man do if sentenced? Go on the blanket, endure the beatings and punishments for years on end, or conform and accept being labelled a criminal?

This new criminalisation policy was tied to a brutal interrogation process in Castlereagh Holding Centre, where people arrested were routinely assaulted by RUC detectives. A 1977 Amnesty International investigation into maltreatment of arrested people in Castlereagh concluded 'that maltreatment of suspected terrorists by the RUC has taken place with sufficient frequency to warrant the establishment of a public inquiry to investigate it.' Amnesty found evidence of systematic physical and psychological assaults, including wrist-bending, hair-pulling, choking, hitting the head off the wall, making people stand for up to four hours, punching and slapping and kicking.

Often, suspects signed confessions. Often, they did not, but the police wrote the confessions 'for' them anyway, a technique called 'verballing'. Bradley cites a couple of examples he knows personally where innocent men went to jail for lengthy periods as a result of such corrupt police practices. One man under interrogation for shooting two policemen got a bad beating by police, who repeatedly demanded to know the names of others involved. Eventually, the man gave the name of his brother-in-law, so as to end the beatings. He knew his brother-in-law was totally innocent and he thought, therefore, could not possibly be charged, let alone convicted. How wrong he was. Both he and his brother-in-law served long sentences for murder.

In another instance, a policeman, Constable Philip Ellis, was shot dead the day after hunger striker Bobby Sands died in May 1981. Ellis, a Scotsman from Kincardine in Fife, was a former British soldier who had joined the RUC in 1980. He was with other police in Duncairn Gardens, the dividing line separating republican New Lodge from loyalist Tiger Bay. There had been ferocious rioting all night and most of the day following Sands's death. The police went to investigate thumping noises at the interface fence screening off the New Lodge, when a shot rang out and Ellis fell dead.

Ellis had been shot by a man called Davy Mackie, according to Bradley one of the best IRA marksmen in Belfast. In training camps in the Republic in the seventies, Mackie had shown unusual natural aptitude with a rifle, being able to split a straw set up as a target at twenty-five metres. He shot Constable Ellis with a single round from a Remington Woodmaster rifle. A local eighteen-year-old was arrested and convicted of the murder and of IRA membership. He had nothing to do with the killing, nor indeed would he have had the marksmanship to carry out the shooting. Bradley says there are 'dozens of such cases in the third batt area alone'.

'It was always hanging over your head. There was always the chance that somebody would name you to get off a hammering themselves. There was always the chance that sometime in Castlereagh they would "verbal" you. You didn't have to sign a confession to get jail. Regularly the cops swore you said it, but then refused to sign, and the judges sent you down anyway.'

There had been lingering hopes among IRA members jailed in the early seventies that 'victory', or a British statement of intent to withdraw, would entail the release of prisoners. By 1976, such hopes had died and people convicted of serious offences had to become reconciled to long years in jail.

The IRA leadership began to take such facts on board. Members were allowed to recognise the courts and fight their cases with counsel, and appeal right through to the highest court possible. Bradley says that by 1976 increasingly heavy sentences were a noticeable feature. A minimum of twenty years for men in a car with a rifle was not unheard of: conspiracy charges were regular and carried a maximum of twenty-five years. IRA members on operations tried to take account of the prospect of huge sentences. People tried to separate themselves from the 'gear' – weapons and explosives – as much as possible. Anyone found with 'gear', even if merely carrying it away from a scene or storing it, was routinely charged with possession 'with intent'.

Bradley was also conscious of a different attitude among British soldiers in 1976 compared to the time before his internment three years earlier. 'They knew they had a fight on their hands. They hadn't beaten the IRA after six years and they knew they weren't going to. They weren't going gung-ho to arrest 'RA men every time they saw them in the street. They knew there was no point. It didn't solve anything. They couldn't intern you. They were starting to play a long game.'

Military intelligence was noticeably much better. 'They let you know they knew you. Each new regiment was introduced to the local IRA. They would stop you in the street and introduce you. They'd bring over the incoming IO [Intelligence Officer] and tell him, "This is Gerry 'Whitey' Bradley".'

Operations became much more difficult. 'After '76, the number of ops dropped dramatically. You couldn't have an op every day. The Brits knew all the tricks by then and who to look out for. You couldn't fire a rifle and run down a street and throw the gun into a house and walk on. Those kinds of ops were over. Houses were well known. The street would be cordoned off before you got out. They knew who they were looking for.

'By 1976 you were worrying about forensics – cleaning up, burning stuff. Also, ops were more selective, not just because of the

Brits, but being careful about civilians. I mean, when everything was going mad in the early seventies, people were getting injured all the time – by accident or bad luck or cross-fire. When the number of ops went way down, you had to watch the background. You had the time to do that and it was the right thing to do. Lots of times, we called off ops to avoid a civilian getting hit.

'There was also major undercover work by the Brits. They had guys in cars and vans. Guys just knocking about the district. It was getting more and more difficult to get ops into the town with the "ring of steel".

'The IRA was different too. The big battalions had gone. It was all "squads", as volunteers called them, "ASUs" as IRA propaganda had it. Men poured out of Long Kesh in 1976, men who had been company commanders, battalion commanders, a lot of top brass. There'd have been about ten former brigade OCs from across the North and sixty staff officers in Long Kesh in 1975. You'd have been blinded by the brass coming out on the streets, but there were not enough places for these guys. Senior republicans were being given the elbow. Guys who were not "yes men" were being got rid of.'

He cites the example of 'Fitzy' from Unity Flats, who had been OC third battalion, and, when interned, OC Long Kesh. 'He was asked to hold gear in his house. Crazy. He had to say no. His house would be raided regularly. The 'RA knew that. It was a device to push him out. When he wouldn't do it, he was dismissed from the army. Another IRA man from the New Lodge, also a former third battalion OC, was beaten up because he refused to lend his car for an operation. How could he? The Brits knew his car. It was going to be stopped at any check point. Didn't matter what story the guys in the car told, it was coming straight back to the guy who owned it.

'Bottom line, BB [Belfast Brigade] and Northern Command, which was set up in 1976, were eliminating local notables. They didn't want any middle management, like battalion OCs or company OCs. It was central control. Brigade operations officer to squads. Battalion OCs were declared redundant, surplus to requirements. Anyway, mostly they were too old to do ops and too well known to the Brits.'

To a large extent, Bradley is describing himself. Belfast Brigade did not want to take on men like Bradley in 1976. They wanted to control the number and nature of operations, not increase them or raise the tempo in a district. In Bradley, they had a former company commander, battalion commander, a hugely experienced operator, but also an awkward customer, ready to question plans and proposals from IRA people he reckoned were not as experienced or as clued-in as himself. He was not afraid to say if he thought something was stupid. He also had a difficult streak of independence, which brigade did not want. That bolshie nature that had got him into trouble with the IRA 'powers that be' in Long Kesh when he was interned, stood against him.

It's only in retrospect that Bradley can see that coming out of Long Kesh in November 1975 and wanting to take up where he'd left off at the end of 1973 was not on. So much had changed. 'It takes time to get adjusted after you come out of prison, get your head round things like new cars, new fashions, crossing the road, even walking up stairs again after a couple of years on the flat. I might have been a danger to myself as well as others if I'd gone straight into action again.'

Apart from their changes in strategy, the reduction in operations and their more selective nature, the Belfast Brigade had valid reasons for not welcoming the wave of men pouring out of Long Kesh. For a start, the security forces obviously had photographs and files on them all. They were what came to be known in later years as 'red lights'. If they were spotted anywhere unusual, they would be immediately questioned, or followed, or lifted. Their very presence could compromise an IRA operation. They could also compromise other men, as yet unknown to army and police, by being seen in their company. They were also out of practice, not having been on the streets in many cases for nearly three years. They were generally older than current IRA operators, and, in the case of some former OCs, a lot older. They might be unwilling to fit into the new squads and take orders from someone younger and perhaps unknown to them.

Naturally, the IRA preferred new, young recruits with no record, known later to the security forces as 'clean skins'. Bradley says recruitment had been dropping off, which suited the IRA leadership, allowing them to be more selective. New recruits had to be coached in the Green Book, the new IRA manual whose rules controlled members' lives. 'People volunteering were warned at length and in detail what they were in for in places like Castlereagh. They were taught anti-interrogation techniques and warned they were likely to end up in jail or dead within six months. It was taking about three months for new recruits to be "Green Booked".'

In Bradley's case, however, all these problems were compounded by the major row he had when he first arrived in Long Kesh, and when he was released it took him a long time to find a place on a squad.

Initially, he was given a job helping out in the Provo club in Unity Flats, but he always considered that as marking time before he got back into action. The IRA was the most important element in his life. He had a lot going for him because he did not fit the usual criteria of someone emerging from Long Kesh. At only twenty-two, he was younger than most former OCs and wasn't demanding to run a squad because of his former seniority. He had lost none of his fitness or his appetite for action, and his experience and reputation still counted. Eventually, in 1978, he was able to join a squad operating in the Lower Falls district, a very dangerous and demanding area with perhaps the heaviest British army presence in the north of Ireland. The other men in the squad were like Bradley: game for anything. Later, as the IRA campaign slowed down in the eighties, a couple of the squad members left to join the INLA (Irish National Liberation Army), dissatisfied with the pace of action and the constraints in the IRA.

The squad's function was to harass the security forces in the Lower Falls, to keep up the tempo of operations, and make life as difficult as possible for the British soldiers in bases like the Conway Mill at North Howard Street, Springfield Road and Divis Flats. It was sporadic rather than regular action. They threw blast bombs at army vehicles emerging from North Howard Street; occasionally, very occasionally, fired at troops and passing security force mobile patrols. Their actions were designed to ensure that the British could never lower their guard because they never knew when they might be attacked. On the other hand, the squad had to be very careful in all their operations that they did not cause any injuries to people in the district, since every person was a potential Sinn Féin supporter.

Even so, despite all the constraints, they were prepared to engage in dare-devil actions. For example, after receiving 'intelligence' that British soldiers were in a hide in the roof space of a derelict house opposite Leeson Street on the Falls Road, Bradley and another member of the squad, Bobby, took a JCB mechanical shovel from a nearby building site and ripped the roof off the house. Luckily for them, the intelligence was wrong on that occasion. British soldiers hiding in the roof space was more a local belief than intelligence based on evidence. Still, they used the same technique of ripping the roof off derelict buildings on more than one occasion because troops had, indeed, been found in such hides. What if there had been soldiers present? It's unlikely that Bradley and his fellow JCB operator would have survived.

Being an IRA member was now no longer a full-time occupation as it had been in the early seventies. Bradley had to earn a living. He learnt a trade, another skill to set beside his military knowledge and expertise. He became a French polisher. He says he had two lives: his married life as a father and worker, and his IRA life – but there was no question in his mind that his IRA life came first and his family took second place. Far down towards the bottom, was his trade.

'I was twenty-one, I think, when I started learning. I must have been the oldest apprentice in the world. Where I learnt the trade was in a government training scheme in west Belfast, but we were all IRA in there. We had guns in the place and could go off to do ops. It was ideal cover. We could come and go as we wanted.

'When I started working after the training scheme, it was never regular – a couple of days work every couple of weeks. I was working for buttons. I mean, I enjoyed doing it. I liked the antiques I was working on. Still do. I appreciate antiques.'

Even working as a French polisher, which took him into 'the houses of the quality' to work on top-class furniture he was an IRA man first and foremost, always 'having a nosey' for opportunities for intelligence useful to the IRA. 'You know, there's a saying, "The Republic doesn't start at nine and end at five."

'I checked photographs on walls and on top of tables, pianos and chests of drawers to see if there was anyone I recognised or anyone in uniform: soldier, UDR, policeman, prison warder, judge, politician. You never knew when you might strike lucky. Then I'd be able to pass the address and details of the house to IRA intelligence. They would try to work out then if it was worth having a go at an op to shoot whoever it was if he fell into any of those categories. You see, the person in the photo mightn't live in the house. Intelligence would have to check all that out.' If it did check out, the person in the house would be classed as 'a legitimate target' in the IRA scheme of things.

On one of his many visits to Castlereagh, a detective kept staring at him during interrogation. Bradley knew why. The detective swore he knew him, apart from his photographs in his file, but could not figure out why he looked familiar. Suddenly, in a flash, it came to him. To his horror, he remembered that Bradley had been working in his house. So the IRA knew where he lived. The detective and his family had to be rehoused immediately.

Such work as Bradley did have was never steady since he regarded his main occupation as being an IRA volunteer. Repeatedly, Bradley remarks how hard the IRA was on its own members, how they were expected to live on a pittance and yet engage incessantly in operations. How was a man supposed to find time to earn enough money to live and keep a family? In the seventies, volunteers got nothing from the IRA except expenses – say, if they needed a taxi to move gear. After all, the war was going to be over in a couple of years so there was no need to make provision for paying volunteers in the longterm.

Later, in the eighties, when it was clear that there was no end in sight for the campaign, an IRA volunteer received £20 a week. That sum remained the same right up to the Good Friday Agreement. That was less than a third of the average industrial wage in 1980 and by the 1990s it was laughable, an impossible sum with which to support a family. To put it in perspective, the average weekly wage in the North in 1998 was around £280. In the seventies, prisoners' families got £5 a week for a married man and £3 a week for a single man from the Prisoners' Dependants' Fund, rising to the giddy heights of £10 and £5 respectively in the 1980s.

Years later, in jail, Bradley listened with astonishment to a senior UVF man, RJ Kerr from Portadown, telling him about burglaries UVF men carried out to keep their families. Robberies IRA men did were carried out only on IRA orders, and the proceeds went into the movement, or else you were in big trouble. Bradley remembers robbing a post-office van with the New Lodge operator, Mickey P. They got about £30,000. The brigade Intelligence Officer came to collect the loot from the call house in Cedar Avenue off the Antrim Road, where Mickey and Bradley were waiting, and saw that Bradley had a hole in the sole of his shoe. He gave him two £5 postal orders out of the robbery's proceeds to buy a pair of shoes. 'Not even cash,' Bradley says indignantly, 'even though there was piles of cash stacked around the room. You'd get some pair of shoes for a tenner, wouldn't you?'

The pittance the IRA provided might have been acceptable to young men in their teens in the early seventies, or when men thought the Troubles would be over quickly. By the end of the seventies, when it was clear the campaign was to be a long haul, IRA men would have to find a way to earn a living. People began to drop out. Apart from a very few at the top, being in the IRA was no longer a full-time activity, even though Bradley insists that as an

IRA man he was 'on the lookout for opportunities twenty-four-seven, always watching for patterns, for wee bits of intelligence'.

There were complications other than money problems. The criminalisation policy was having a huge impact on the republican movement. As more and more IRA men and women were convicted and went into the 'blocks' (or in the case of women into Armagh prison) and 'on the blanket', Bradley says 'the momentum moved towards the prisoners'. The emphasis came off operations and into agitation in support of the anti H-block campaign. Every republican district in the North and many towns in the Irish Republic had H-block committees, initially known as Relatives' Action committees. Bradley was on the H-block committee in Unity Flats. It took up a lot of time and energy. But he was frustrated at the lack of military action. He was 'army' first and foremost and didn't want to get sidelined into political stuff. This sort of agitation was not what he was interested in. He went once on an H-block march from Newry to Dublin. It took three days. Even though in the end there were about 30,000-40,000 people walking through Dublin, this experience convinced him that marches were a complete waste of time – walking along, with banners and posters condemning Maggie Thatcher, chanting, 'Maggie, Maggie, Maggie, out, out, out!' Pointless, humiliating. He vowed he would never do that again.

As the anti-H-block campaign became more and more desperate into 1980, and then culminated in the hunger strikes of 1981, Bradley and men like him became more and more furious at being held back. He admits he could see how the H-block campaign showed republicans how to organise people and politicise them. 'Everyone in the districts was united, the first time since 1971. There were people at protests who had never been at one before. There was total organisation of each district. Once again, the women came in and came to the forefront as committee members. They didn't just make tea and sandwiches. In a lot of places they ran the show.'

Instructions from the IRA leadership were to tone down operations while hunger strikers were dying in order not to distract from the political strength of their case. Any operations that went wrong and caused civilian casualties could seriously undermine the demand for political status, which was the prisoners' original stance. Instead, the IRA in local districts concentrated on organising riots when men died. 'It was ridiculous. On the day Bobby Sands died, you had senior IRA men out throwing petrol bombs with kids. They looked stupid. The Brits were firing thousands of plastic bullets into the crowds, hitting people, killing people. We had the gear, hundreds of rifles, but we couldn't open up. I disagreed with "no ops" during the hunger strike. If I'd been on hunger strike, I'd have wanted to carry on the war. It was a shame the IRA didn't go into action in some way.'

That attitude may have prevailed in Belfast, where rioting was endemic during the summer of 1981 as hunger strikers died, though, in fact, a number of soldiers and police were shot dead in Belfast in 1981. In rural areas, however, there was no let-up in IRA attacks, and the IRA killed a substantial number of members of the security forces in this period, including five soldiers in a single 500kg landmine explosion in Camlough, south Armagh.

But the riots and mass demonstrations did serve their purpose. The British government deployed units like the Royal Marines in Belfast, who, like the Parachute Regiment, had a reputation for gratuitous violence. The army's response to rioting was to fire huge numbers of plastic bullets – over 20,000 in Belfast alone – killing a number of innocent people, including Nora McCabe, who was one of a group of women saying the rosary in a street in west Belfast in the aftermath of the death of a hunger striker Joe McDonnell. Her family was later awarded over £25,000 compensation. Two young girls, aged fourteen and eleven, one carrying home a bottle of milk, were also killed by plastic bullets. The behaviour of the British soldiers, the reckless and in some cases malicious firing of plastic bullets, succeeded in politicising another generation who had not experienced the traumatic events of 1969-71.

Bradley was psychologically badly affected by the hunger strikes and developed an intense personal hatred for Prime Minister Margaret Thatcher. During his time in Long Kesh, he had been in the same hut as one of the hunger strikers who died, Kieran Doherty. He had known Doherty at secondary school, CBS on the Glen Road, where he had been a couple of years behind Bradley. Doherty died in August 1981 on his seventy-third day on hunger strike. He had been elected to the Dáil as TD for Cavan–Monaghan while on hunger strike. Bradley says

Doherty was like him – not political, an army man. He had no time for talks and ceasefires and easing back.

Little did Bradley and IRA men like him know that the republican leadership had been as stunned as any observers by their political success in 1981, with Bobby Sands being elected to Westminster while on hunger strike with over 30,000 votes, and H-block candidates topping the poll in many district council elections. It was a political earthquake. The general belief among IRA men like Bradley was that there would be renewed vigour in the IRA campaign once the prison issue was resolved, but they were wrong.

Men like Gerry Adams quickly realised that 1981 was a watershed which demonstrated that there was a huge republican constituency to be garnered in the North if it was handled properly. Slowly, but surely, the republican leadership would reel in the IRA, all the time assuring volunteers that the campaign was continuing unabated and that new materiel was coming in for a big push. From 1981 on, Sinn Féin candidates, not surrogates supporting prisoners or claiming to be independent republicans, would participate in any elections. Danny Morrison, Sinn Féin's Director of Publicity, famously told the party's *ardfheis* in autumn 1981 that 'with a ballot box in one hand and an Armalite in the other we can take power in Ireland.' Though few in the IRA saw it at the time, that policy inevitably meant that the IRA would have to pay attention not to injure the political ambitions of a burgeoning Sinn Féin.

7

BACK TO BUSINESS

'I was still acting very cocky when I arrived in Castlereagh.
Didn't feel it, though, but you had to keep up appearances. I knew my
way around so well I was even leading my police escort along the
corridors, turning corners I was familiar with, until the escort said,
"No, not that way." It wasn't long before I found out what was
different. Charlie McKiernan was brought into my cell and identified me
as a member of the squad that had carried out the bombing.'

By the end of August 1981 ten men were dead and the hunger strikes were called off, mainly as a result of families intervening when men fell into a coma. The IRA could get back to operations again. They had plenty of new recruits and plenty of gear, and plenty of experienced men anxious for action after a year of frustration. At the end of the year, a squad asked Bradley to help with logistics in an operation that would have a profound effect on his life.

Operations were becoming increasingly difficult and dangerous, with all the complications already described: forensics, surveillance, ubiquitous helicopters, the security forces' more sophisticated understanding of IRA methods, quicker reaction by police and army, fewer opportunities because of better field craft by the security forces. Therefore, while operations became less frequent, they tended to become larger set-pieces, the planning and execution of which were lengthy and painstaking and meticulous.

'You had to plan weeks ahead, maybe have an op on the shelf waiting for the right circumstances, maybe almost do a dry run. You had to time ops to perfection: how long it took to walk a certain distance, drive a certain distance; plan the run back, make sure you could get the clothes washed or burnt, get a shower. You learned about putting plugs in your ears for powder residue, to wear gloves, a boiler suit, just cover up and then destroy everything you had on – all that. Just going out shooting was out of the question.'

There was another hazard. With the end of internment in 1975 and the emphasis on criminalisation, convictions had become paramount. However, the initial drive in the late seventies involving brutal interrogation methods, and questionable confessions had produced such a barrage of international criticism, including cases at the European Court of Human Rights, that the security forces began to look for other methods of gaining convictions. They hit on supergrasses. 'Supergrass' was a term taken from the English underworld, where someone who gave evidence against an accomplice was known as a 'grass'. The period immediately after the hunger strikes, 1981-82, was the peak of the so-called 'supergrass' arrests, when self-confessed IRA members (and loyalist UVF members too) were granted immunity from prosecution in return for providing complete details of all they knew about the IRA. Some were also given a new identity and a new life in a different country. The first, and most notorious, supergrass was Christopher Black from Ardoyne, who gave evidence against over forty alleged IRA members and auxiliaries.

In the early eighties, the tactic caused consternation among the IRA in Belfast and Derry. After Black's disclosures, no district seemed immune, including, it seemed, Unity Flats.

The IRA in Unity Flats had observed that on Friday nights and Saturdays the RUC regularly stationed a Land Rover of police at the Peter's Hill corner of the Unity complex to cover the possibility of clashes between residents of Unity and loyalists passing on their way to and from the Shankill Road. Experience had shown that, with groups of football fans on the move, Saturday was the most likely day for such clashes, and that is why a static patrol was placed there. Police commanders regarded the position as relatively safe since the vehicle they deployed was 'hard-skinned', meaning it could withstand rifle shots.

The IRA had also noticed that the Land Rover was always parked as far back as possible from the road, close against a fence, to leave the footpath mostly clear. A squad decided to plant a bomb, powerful enough to destroy the armoured vehicle, behind the fence. It would be possible to run a command wire from Unity Flats to the bomb, which could then be detonated by line of sight – that is to say, when the Land Rover was lined up with a particular point. Using the command wire instead of a radio-controlled bomb would also mean that electronic counter measures could not be used to prevent detonation.

The plans were carefully laid and the bomb was placed hours before the police took up their familiar position. It was 21 November 1981. The police Land Rover arrived on cue, but did not park in the usual place. After hours of waiting and watching, the squad had to remove the bomb, dismantle the wiring, store the bomb and weapons safely in dumps, and go home. The following Saturday they would try again.

About three days before they tried again, one of the squad, Charlie McKiernan, was arrested and taken to Castlereagh, not an unusual occurrence for an IRA man. 'The question for us was: would he break? Would he tell the police about the planned operation? Normally, the operation would have been called off – should have been called off. On balance, the squad – Beef, JC, Spud, 'Wee Gerard' and a man the Brits called "Nutter" – decided McKiernan would be okay and, anyway, if he was still in Castlereagh when the bomb exploded, he had a cast-iron alibi, so why would he say anything?' The operation went ahead.

The following Saturday, 28 November, the IRA repeated the operation. This time the Land Rover turned up as normal and took its usual position at the fence, on the other side of which a bomb now lay concealed. The same Land Rover crew did not sit on station all afternoon, but were relieved after a few hours. The IRA waited for the change-over. As another Land Rover with a replacement crew drew up beside the first one, the IRA detonated the bomb. Constable William Coulter was killed instantly as he was about to get into the static Land Rover. Other police were injured and the two vehicles destroyed.

'I knew I would be lifted the next morning. So did several other IRA men in Unity. It would have been strange if we hadn't been. There was no point in going into hiding because that would have been tantamount to admitting guilt, and the security forces would have begun a manhunt. Better to wait and take the medicine. So I was waiting. I had matches in the turn-ups of my jeans so I could have a smoke of my roll-ups in Castlereagh. I was wearing slip-on shoes because they took your laces away. I was resigned to seven days in the holding centre where I had been umpteen times before. I would just sit it out.

'As I expected, the police and army came for me next morning, but when I was brought out of my home in Unity and saw all the jeeps and soldiers covering the RUC arrest team, I realised I was the only man being lifted. There was something different going on. True, the squad was not from Unity, but why were no other IRA people in Unity being scooped? An RUC man said, "We've got you this time, you bastard."

'I was still acting very cocky when I arrived in Castlereagh. Didn't feel it, though, but you had to keep up appearances. I knew my way around so well I was even leading my police escort along the corridors, turning corners I was familiar with until the escort said, "No, not that way." It wasn't long before I found out what was different. Charlie McKiernan was brought into my cell and identified me as a member of the squad that had carried out the bombing.'

McKiernan's appearance in the cell had a terrible effect on Bradley. He was thunderstruck. There then followed what Bradley describes as the worst seven days ever in Castlereagh.

His chief interrogator – big, coarse-featured, with long black hair – reminded him of the 1970s Romanian tennis professional, Ilie Năstase, noted for his histrionics on court and given to sudden outbursts of irrational behaviour – sometimes deliberately affected, sometimes not. It was impossible to tell. Bradley's interrogator had been hit on the head with a brick in Unity Flats in August 1969. He claimed that he got so much compensation that he was able to buy a house. 'I reckon there's no way he should have been allowed to stay in the police. I reckon he'd been brain-damaged. He was just maniacal, a complete psycho. He had it in for me because I was from Unity where he'd got his head injury twelve years before.

'The first thing he did when he came in with another detective was to take his coat off and hang it over the CCTV camera in the room. I was sure I was going to get a battering. I wasn't going to take it lying down. As soon as "Năstase" approached, I jumped up and took a swing at him. I stood up to them, shouting, "C'mon, you bastards."' Bradley says his body was generating so much adrenalin and testosterone that his leading leg in his boxing stance developed a tremor, which seems to have alarmed the police. They had a clear sense that if it came to it, the adrenalin would instantly be rerouted from the leg to Bradley's fists and feet. Although they were both much bigger than Bradley, they immediately backed away from him, one saying, 'Jesus, look at his leg.' They both started saying soothing words. 'Now come on, Gerald, calm down now, take it easy.' The two big men backing off amused Bradley, who did calm down. He did not get a 'battering'. There would have been no point. McKiernan had probably told the police all there was to know.

In the course of the relentless interrogations, Bradley adopted a response which he quickly regretted. 'The Castlereagh interrogators usually would not let a man sit at the table, but pulled him up and made him stand, to tire him out. They could also push you around when you were standing and land no-warning blows. Sometimes men lay down on the floor, but they risked being kicked or stamped on or stood on.' Bradley decided to stand up of his own accord and stand to attention, staring ahead. Why he did this, he cannot explain. He admits 'it was not the smartest move', but maybe it was an act of defiance. 'Năstase' came behind him and leaned on his shoulders for ages at a time, shouting into his ears and heaving his body around.

'There were four interrogations a day. Sometimes they would bring you back to your cell at 2.00am. They kept the lights on all the time. It was difficult to sleep. I was exhausted from standing to attention, with "Năstase" lying across my shoulders, yelling and lurching his weight around. I did my best to show I was not perturbed by the interrogations. I ate all the food they presented and tried to stay outwardly calm, but inside I was in turmoil – shocked, wrecked about McKiernan's treachery.

'The police showed me massive blown-up photographs of the destruction the bomb did, the wounded men lying beside the vehicle, the dead policeman. They shoved my head down at the photos, they screamed at me about the death and injuries. None of it had the slightest effect on me. I couldn't care less about blown-up Land-Rovers; that's what the IRA was supposed to be doing. It was a success. They used to try this "remorse" stuff and, even more ridiculous, religion stuff – you know: you'll go to hell, why don't you repent, accept your Saviour, see the light, all this stuff. Might have worked on loyalists. Only one 'RA man I ever heard of was affected by it, but he also got a hammering, so it's hard to tell which worked.

'What did have an effect was standing for hours with mad "Năstase" bearing down on my shoulders, and worrying all the time about what Charlie McKiernan might have told the police. After a couple of days, I was worn out. I was at my wit's end. I decided to take a leaf out of the book of the blanket men. I went to the toilet and smeared crap all over the back of my long hair and on the back of my neck and collar. When the next interrogation session began, and "Năstase" took up his usual position lying across my shoulders, he suddenly stood up, smelling his hands and sleeves, and shouted, "You dirty bastard." That put an end to that particular approach to questioning.

'In the end, there was nothing against me except McKiernan's evidence, but that was enough for me to be charged with murder and several explosives offences. I was remanded in custody.'

During his months in custody in 1982, as the case against him and the four other men charged was being prepared, it emerged that the RUC CID (Criminal Intelligence Department) had known about the plan to attack the Land Rover crew but, incredibly, had let the attack go ahead. As these details became known, the Police Federation (the police union) gave vent to furious protests that CID had not warned the uniformed police of the impending attack. The whole incident became a *cause célèbre*. The widow of Constable Coulter received substantial undisclosed damages from the Northern Ireland Office. It still remains a mystery why senior police allowed the attack to take place without tampering with the bomb. They knew where it was because Charlie McKiernan had told them where it was being stored from the previous week. He had watched the IRA man taking the bomb to the dump. Why did they not arrest the IRA men as they planted the bomb, or after they had planted the bomb, but before it was detonated? They were going to charge them solely on McKiernan's testimony anyway. Who or what were CID protecting? Another informer? Certainly not the police in the Land Rovers.

In the event, McKiernan withdrew his evidence, refused to testify and the case collapsed. He was later convicted of two killings carried out in the months before the Unity Flats' bomb and served a lengthy jail sentence. Obviously, the police had offered him some kind of deal about the murder charges, perhaps even immunity, if he would turn Queen's evidence, or, as it was called at the time, 'turn supergrass' against the IRA in Unity. Whatever deal the police had offered, it clearly was not enough. Or perhaps McKiernan did not know enough to qualify for supergrass status on the scale of Christopher Black, who named scores of people in north Belfast.

Indeed, it transpired that it was because of Black's information that Charlie McKiernan had been arrested. No doubt it was when police confronted McKiernan with Black's information about the recent killings McKiernan had been involved in, that he caved in and told what he knew about the local IRA. Police in Castlereagh told Bradley that if he had not been arrested in connection with the bomb at Peter's Hill, he too was going to be arrested on foot of information from Black.

Members of other illegal organisations followed suit, with super-grasses also emerging from the ranks of the UVF and INLA in 1982. It is clear that the police thought McKiernan would enable them to mop up the IRA in Unity Flats, just as Christopher Black had done in Ardoyne and the Bone.

Although Bradley was a free man after McKiernan's retraction, his arrest, the shock of being named by McKiernan, his interrogation and the long period of anxiety while remanded in custody left an indelible mark on him. He seems almost to have had a nervous breakdown. His hair fell out after he was released in 1982 around the time of his twenty-eighth birthday. He was a marked man, receiving threats from police when they stopped him.

Three or four days after his release from remand in Crumlin Road jail, as he walked up to the jail with a friend to collect his personal effects, Bradley had a furious, hysterical confrontation with police at Carlisle Circus, where he says he was so unbalanced he almost frightened himself. A police Land Rover drew up, and police got out and stopped him. 'One cop came over and said: "Listen, we're not gonna charge you next time. We're gonna whack you." I just lost it. "You're gonna whack me? You're a marked man. I know you. You're gonna die in a Land Rover. I'm gonna make sure you get blown up and your mates here – the lot of you ..." and so on. You could see the shock on his face. Other times, police would stop me and say they were gonna gave my name to loyalists as a target, ask for me to be done. "We'll get you done," they'd say. Every time they saw me, they were at it. I was just full of anger and contempt for the cops.'

Given his state of mind when he came out of jail, Bradley asked the Belfast Brigade OC for a break from the IRA until he got his head clear, but he was refused. Why, he does not know. 'Maybe they were short of men in the third batt area after Black?' Bradley took the break anyway. He could not go on. 'I had been at it twenty-four/seven for years. British soldiers do a tour of four months, or whatever it is, and then get rotated. Afterwards, if they get into a fight in a pub in England or go off the rails some way, they go to court and their defence says, "He was in Northern Ireland and he was under a lot of stress" and all that. And the judge says, "Okay." If you were in the IRA in Belfast you never got a break, year after year. Guys like Dan Breen were at it max three years. We'd been operating since 1970. Nobody had ever done anything like it.'

Mentally, Bradley was not ready to go back into action, and, in reality, he was not much use to the IRA. Apart from the fact that his nerves were shattered by his experiences in Castlereagh and by the threat of a life sentence as a result of supergrass evidence being used against him, the police kept harassing him. 'Things were very hot in 1982. The police were raging about me, making threats when they saw me. They were constantly after me.' The case against Bradley had been dropped, but as far as police in Belfast were concerned, Bradley was guilty. He felt he was not safe walking down the street. He was going to be 'gripped' (arrested and taken to Castlereagh) any time he was seen on a street. That was not a new experience. He had been repeatedly 'gripped' since 1972, but his nerves were shattered now and he could not take it. He decided to make a complete break. He followed the route of scores of other republicans. He went to America. Little did he know that America would be even more dangerous to his health than Belfast ever was.

He flew to New York from Dublin. He was genuinely looking for a break from the IRA. He wanted to work, to make some money. The east-coast cities of the USA, from Boston south to Philadelphia, were full of northern republicans in 1982, men who had emigrated, often temporarily, after completing a prison sentence or being released from internment. Like everyone else, Bradley had heard stories of the money you could make in America. In New York he shared an apartment with three other republicans and looked for work, a search which proved more difficult than he had been led to believe. At nights, he socialised in Irish bars, mainly with republicans from the North, especially from Belfast.

'I hadn't got a bean. Basically the guys let me stay in the apartment and kept me while I looked for work. I wasn't a heavy drinker. Never was. A couple of drinks would do me, but other guys insisted on buying me drinks. That's the way it was. Your own countrymen looked after you when you went to America. Same with Italians or anybody else.'

One Sunday, after two or three weeks in New York, Bradley was in a bar called the Hideaway in Woodside, an Irish area in the Queens district. There were several Belfast men in the bar. An argument developed between one of the Belfast men, Liam McGowan, and an Irish-American called Ron, who was a New York police cadet. There had been previous ill-feeling between Ron and McGowan about a girl. After words between the two and a scuffle, the management decided to eject Ron. As he was going, he rained insults on the assembled company, shouting 'Irish bastards' and 'Belfast bastards'.

Ron remained outside, shouting abuse. Others in the bar urged McGowan to go out and 'have a fair go' to settle it, but he refused. 'If he'd had a pair of balls, three men wouldn't have got shot.' Although, strictly speaking it was none of Bradley's business, he took exception to Ron's behaviour and got antagonised by his insults to the company and he went out of the bar to Ron. Everyone had drink taken. Bradley is the first to admit that in those days he had a quick temper with drink taken, and a volatile response to insults and abuse.

Though not very tall, Bradley is very powerfully built, was always very fit and a formidable boxer. Bradley had started boxing when he was twelve or thirteen in a club in west Belfast, and he honed his skills whenever he could, though he wasn't a success in the ring. 'I only had two or three fights. I was what they call a bleeder.' Even to this day, in his fifties, he keeps it up and does many rounds in the gym every day. He was often quick to put his skills to use. 'I had all the small man's vices,' he says. Bradley set about Ron and gave the much bigger police cadet 'a bit of a battering'. Satisfied, Bradley went back into the bar and resumed drinking.

Half an hour later, Ron was back. He could be heard outside, shouting through a window, challenging Bradley to a fight – a challenge Bradley was hardly likely to refuse, having already beaten Ron and having had a couple more drinks. He and a couple of others, Mickey Quigley and Mickey McGloin, went out to Ron, who pulled a gun. Bradley hit him instantly and Ron ran off, firing two shots. As Bradley says, at this stage of the evening he was 'well--oiled', otherwise he would not have done what he did next. With the other two, he chased Ron, ducking and diving between cars. Bradley smiles ruefully as he recalls holding up a metal bin lid he had snatched up as a shield because Ron was firing repeatedly at his pursuers. As Bradley is well aware, his bin lid was as much use as a chocolate fireguard when it came to stopping bullets.

It turned out that Ron had two guns. He fired eight or nine shots. Quigley and Bradley ran along one street after him while McGloin ran down a parallel street to head Ron off. As Quigley got to the end of the street, he was shot in the arm. McGloin arrived, was lightly grazed by another bullet, but went to the aid of Quigley, who was lying on the ground. Bradley came on the scene and ran at Ron, who shot him in the stomach at point-blank range, badly wounding him. The bullet was a .38, luckily low-velocity, which did not tumble, but nevertheless was a big enough calibre to cause serious injury. It was like getting hit by a train.

Bradley remembers using his elbows to crawl towards the doorway of another bar, bleeding and gasping for help, but the doorman casually closed the doors. An ambulance arrived some time later – he has no idea how long – and took Bradley to a hospital in Queens. He had massive internal injuries, which required immediate surgery. He lost his spleen and a kidney, and had permanent damage done to his bowel tract. He was lucky in that if you're going to be shot, New York is a good place for it to happen. Surgeons are used to dealing with bullet wounds and their consequences. All the doctors who dealt with Bradley in later years have testified that the surgeon did a brilliant job. He saved Bradley's life.

'It was a sort of welfare hospital. They'd work on you even if you hadn't insurance, which I didn't. Pretty rough place. They dealt with convicts from a jail nearby. There were guys with leg-irons on in bed, others chained to the bed. The good side was that a lot of top doctors came in and worked *pro bono*. I was lucky.'

As for Ron, in the cold light of dawn when he had sobered up, he gave himself up and was arrested. However, Bradley would not press charges, so Ron walked free. Furthermore, since Bradley would not go to court, he could not claim compensation. 'I wouldn't send anyone to jail. I've been in jail four times. I'd only been in three times then, but I wouldn't put anyone in. I wouldn't point anyone out in court.' Ron's family gathered together some money, about $3,000, and gave it to Bradley, but it didn't even get near the cost of the hospital treatment. The hospital was used to having people leave without paying, as Bradley did.

As soon as he was able, after about three weeks, Bradley left hospital and flew back to Dublin in great discomfort. He could barely walk. There had been wild rumours in Belfast about what had happened to him. Everyone knew he'd been shot, but people had embroidered the how and why: there had been a gun battle with New York police; an arms deal had gone wrong; he'd been fighting over a woman; the IRA had shot him. Bradley went back to Belfast to put the record straight, but the Belfast Brigade OC advised him to leave. There was a fear that the police would arrest him, hold him on some trumped-up charge, beat him up and deliberately open his wounds, damage him so that he was permanently disabled. He left Belfast and spent some time in a caravan in the town of Omeath, just south of the border, still recovering. He moved into a room in the Imperial hotel in Dundalk to 'get some heat', but it cost a fortune, so he was back in the caravan after two days. It took ages to recuperate. He was walking bent double for weeks. He was in constant pain. For a variety of reasons, therefore, he was certainly no use to the IRA in Belfast.

As soon as he felt able, he flew back to America. Despite his terrible experience, he had enjoyed a freedom there he had never felt before in his life. He did not have to look over his shoulder all the time. He was literally carefree: no Brits, no police, no personal-security problems. He wanted to give it another go, this time for good: a new life. He persuaded his wife to accompany him, so they gave up their home in Unity Flats and the family flew out to the USA.

However, although he was out of the formal IRA organisation because of his injuries and the events following the killing of Constable Coulter, the IRA saw ways he could help them out – and the IRA always had first call on Bradley's loyalties. When they learned he was going back to America, a member of Belfast Brigade staff called Fitzy approached him and asked him to do a bit of work for them in the States. He told Bradley that although they had 'loads of weapons', the IRA needed spares, especially main recoil springs and magazines. Could he arrange something? Bradley promised to do his best. Back in America, he soon met Gabriel McGahey socially. The press had given McGahey the grandiose title of 'OC America'.

McGahey's main job in the US, as it had been since the seventies when he was living in Southampton and collecting Armalites off the *QE2*, was gun-running. The FBI called McGahey 'Mr Panicky', because it was clear he was aware he was being watched. McGahey had known he was a marked man and had been trying to cover his tracks when he was caught in an FBI 'sting' trying to buy Redeye surface-to-air missiles. Although he knew he was under surveillance, Bradley says, 'He took the chance because the Redeyes were so important to the IRA given the damage helicopters were doing to operations.' In 1983 McGahey was out on $1 million bail, charged with attempting to procure Redeye missiles.

Bradley got on well with McGahey, or 'McGack' as he calls him. McGahey was originally from Ardoyne, so there was much he and Bradley had in common – shared acquaintances and shared memories of places. For a time, they lived in the same building and Bradley did some 'jobs' for him. On one occasion, McGahey sent him to collect IRA money, thousands of dollars he was owed from a man living in upstate New York. The man had bought M16 rifles with the IRA's money, but had sold them and claimed the rifles had been stolen from him. He refused to pay the money back or accept the debt.

An American woman, who was a vociferous IRA supporter, drove Bradley upstate to the house. She sat chatting amicably to the man's wife while Bradley had the man by the throat in another room, assuring him his days were numbered. But nothing Bradley said or did would convince him he had to pay. He told Bradley to send McGahey up with a gun and they could have it out in a field. It conjures up images of Tombstone or Dodge City in the nineteenth century. Bradley reckons the would-be gunfighter would not have lasted ten seconds with 'McGack'. However, his bail conditions meant that McGahey could not leave New York city, which was why he had sent Bradley, so the swindler remained safe for the time being.

Altogether, Bradley spent about fourteen months in New York. He travelled back and forth several times through Dublin, usually on a false passport. Like thousands of Irish, he also had a false US social security number to enable him to work. In the early eighties, New York was a playground for Irish republicans. Bradley was amazed at the freedom they enjoyed and the open support they had from prominent American politicians, businessmen and television and media stars. It was startling for him to see Irish-Americans wearing baseball caps and T-shirts in public with 'Up the RA' or 'All the way, IRA' emblazoned on them. One well-educated, well-to-do woman, who occasionally drove Bradley around on 'jobs', wore her own bespoke metal badge on her blouse, proclaiming her to be a member of the 'American IRA'.

One of America's biggest soap stars, Carroll O'Connor, who played Archie Bunker in *All in the Family* – the equivalent of Alf Garnett in BBC's *Till Death Us Do Part* – was a fervent republican supporter. *All in the Family* was based in Queens in New York. Gerry Bradley had his family with him for the New York St Patrick's Day parade in 1983 and Carroll O'Connor marched behind him, as did New York Governor Mario Cuomo and Mayor Ed Koch. Old IRA man and founder member of Noraid, Mike Flannery, led the parade as Grand Marshal down Fifth Avenue four months after he was acquitted of arms smuggling. Bradley walked for a while behind Flannery at the head of the parade, gaping at the famous Americans who were participating.

He was even interviewed for US radio. He was asked his opinion of Flannery's controversial appointment as Grand Marshal, which had led to some prominent Irish-Americans, including Terence Cardinal Cooke and Senator Daniel P. Moynihan, to boycott the parade. 'I told the radio Flannery was a great guy, highly regarded in Ireland and that I'd flown out specially from Belfast to be on the parade because Flannery was Grand Marshal.'

There were constant Noraid functions where Irish-Americans met IRA men and heard their stories. These functions each raised hundreds of thousands of dollars, much of it in cash. A favourite at such functions was Joe Cahill, former IRA chief of staff. 'The Yanks loved Joe Cahill. They loved to hear his stories. They all knew about his history and his reputation going back to the forties. They wanted to hear it from him. Cahill raised millions. Cahill was a regular visitor to New York on false passports long before the visa controversy of 1994. He was in and out of America loads of times before 1994. He was just an old guy. Nobody paid any attention to him at customs.' The visa controversy is a reference to President Bill Clinton's decision in 1994, against his own State Department's advice and strong British objections, to give Cahill a visa to visit the USA to convince Irish-Americans that an IRA ceasefire was a good idea. It was probably the only time Cahill visited America legally.

As treasurer of the republican movement, Cahill would collect the cash and cheques at Noraid functions and take them away in a plastic bag. 'There was this old guy [Cahill was born in 1920] walking along in baggy clothes, wearing a cap and carrying a crumply plastic bag. Nobody would have guessed it held, maybe, a couple of hundred thousand dollars. He walked. He took the subway. Cahill wouldn't take a taxi. He reckoned it was a waste of money.' Afterwards, he would deposit the money or arrange for it to be taken to Canada or on flights to Ireland from the USA, converted into traveller's cheques, or even in people's carry-on luggage.

For Bradley in America, there was as much IRA activity as there was at home, though of a different nature. He had wanted a break from the IRA, was even prepared to leave it and start afresh with his family in America, but found himself, as he says, 'helping out'. He carried messages, maintained connections between Belfast and Noraid people, and tried to 'get gear'. That was one area where he failed. As he says: 'It was easy to get gear. People came up to you and offered guns, all kind of guns. The problem was getting them back home. The Feds watched everything. Took photos. Filmed. By 1983 they had fairly well broken up the gun-running.' Thanks to Margaret Thatcher's good relations with President Ronald Reagan, the heat was on the IRA in America. The following year, 1984, an FBI undercover operation led to the capture of seven tons of weaponry aboard an Irish trawler, the *Marita Ann*, after the cargo had been transferred at sea from a Boston fishing ship, the *Valhalla*.

Carrying messages was easier, but it had its own risks. Once, travelling to New York on his own passport, Bradley was taken aside at immigration into a room where there was a man with a huge ledger on a table in front of him. The official ran his finger down the ledger and came to Bradley's name. 'You are Gerald "Whitey" Bradley, a member of the Provisional IRA,' he said. He was going to deny him entry to the US. But Bradley denied the accusation. He said he was indeed Gerry Bradley, but it was a common name in Ireland; that must be someone different. 'No,' the official insisted. 'You have the same date of birth.' He became more and more irate at Bradley's denials and was threatening to take Bradley away and strip-search him, a worrying development as Bradley was carrying important letters from the IRA to people in America sewn into the lining of his jacket.

Bradley denied he had the same date of birth. The official kept repeating the American dating system saying, 'Your date of birth is five, three, 1954.' Bradley said no, it was 'three, five' in the British system, and that's what it said in his passport – it must be a mistake – it was someone else – somebody had mixed up the dating. In the middle of the dispute another, more senior official walked by and the man with the ledger asked for guidance. After looking at Bradley and listening to his point about the day/month order, the senior man said, 'Let him go.' A close shave.

Bradley learnt from such experiences. First rule, don't be a lone man because you're likely to be picked out for a 'random' search or inquiry. He learned to attach himself to a woman with children. Help her to carry bags or load her trolley and push it. Keep your head down. Read something. Be inconspicuous. Talk to a priest – there's always one on a flight. Walk along with him. Off a flight to Boston, Bradley linked up with an Irish priest and ended up travelling with him in a taxi to the house where he lived with other priests. After some conversation with the priest, Bradley decided it was safe to tell him he was in the IRA and on IRA business. The priest brought him down to the basement to meet an old priest. It turned out that the Black and Tans had shot the old priest's brother in 1920. Next day, one of the priests drove Bradley to the train station for the New York train and gave him an address to go to if he was ever 'stuck in New York'.

In the event, Bradley never was 'stuck in New York', though sometimes he was stuck for steady work. He could always find jobs – casual, short-term – on building sites, doing repair work. He worked for a while in the notorious 'Tombs', the New York prison where Joe Doherty from the New Lodge district of north Belfast was held for years pending extradition proceedings to Belfast for his involvement in shooting a British SAS officer. None of it was particularly hard or demanding work, which was just as well because Bradley, as he says, 'was still not himself' after his gunshot wounds.

In one sense, his time in America proved useful in that it did provide a peaceful interlude for his recovery, free from the stresses of Belfast. It was clear he was not going to make his fortune in New York. 'I could never get a good, permanent job. I was always stuck with jobs paying the minimum wage. You could get building work and casual jobs, but nothing to keep a family on.' Bradley's wife hated New York and wanted to go home. 'I ran into a brick wall. Couldn't get well-paid work. I was on a false social security number.

Couldn't get the kids into school: "Are they US citizens? No. Bring their birth certificates." How could I?' He and his wife would have been exposed as illegals, overstaying their time. His wife and children returned to Belfast, leaving him in New York. By 1984 it was time for him to go home for good. He and his wife rented a maisonette in Unity Flats. He reckoned he was fit to play a role in the IRA in Belfast again.

8

OPERATING AGAINST THE ODDS

'I was ready to go out there and get myself killed. I feel so betrayed by
what happened, the way it happened and the way they lied to us
over the years ... There was to be no decommissioning ...
In fact, they were waiting for the right moment to destroy
all the gear and put the IRA out of business.
If they'd kept the IRA strong, they'd have got a lot more
out of the Brits than they settled for in 1998.'

On the morning of 12 July 1920, after a night spent attacking
Rearcross RIC barracks in north Tipperary, a column of fifty IRA
men commanded by Sean Treacy and Ernie O'Malley were marching four abreast through the village of Hollyford, ten kilometres as
the crow flies from Rearcross. In his memoir *My Fight for Irish Freedom*, Dan Breen recalls that 'all the villagers turned out and
shouted, "Up Sinn Féin!". O'Malley exclaimed, "O holy mackerel,
do you hear what they are calling us, Bloody Sinn Féiners?"' IRA
men like Breen and O'Malley regarded Sinn Féin as a purely political organisation, very much second fiddle to the IRA. Admittedly,

Sinn Féin acquired some legitimacy for the IRA by confirming its electoral support, but for IRA men it certainly did not contribute directly to the war against the British or advance Irish independence. Many in the IRA regarded Sinn Féin with the same degree of suspicion they reserved for all politicians. This attitude extended as far up the ranks as Michael Collins, who tried to ensure that when candidates for the 1918 general election were being selected care should be taken to avoid 'men of the compromising type'. Ironically, by December 1921 when it came to ratifying the Treaty, he could have done with more men of 'the compromising type'.

There is an uncanny similarity between the attitude displayed by the IRA towards Sinn Féin in the years 1919 to 1922 and the antipathy among many IRA men in the 1980s towards the developing importance of Sinn Féin in the republican movement. This antipathy came to a head in 1985 when senior men in the Belfast IRA were court-martialled and dismissed from the IRA. One of them was Ivor Bell, who had appointed Gerry Bradley OC of Belfast's third battalion in 1973. By 1985, Bell was a former Belfast Brigade commander, former chief of staff and former member of the Army Council. Bell and a few leading Belfast IRA men had tried to prevent funds being diverted from the IRA towards preparations for the 1985 council elections, but the Adams leadership was firmly in control and they failed. It is clear now that the politicians in the movement were in the ascendant because the expulsion of Bell and a couple of other respected IRA operators was accepted by the wider movement without a ripple.

The increasing emphasis on electoral politics after 1981 was changing the republican movement out of all recognition. Sinn Féin stood in assembly elections in autumn 1982 and polled 64,000 votes. In the 1983 British general election, the party polled over 100,000 votes and Gerry Adams was elected Member of Parliament (MP) for West Belfast. Danny Morrison came within a whisker, 78 votes, of defeating the DUP MP Willie McCrea in Mid-Ulster. For the first time, republicans entertained the possibility of overtaking the SDLP and becoming the majority voice of northern nationalists. In 1985 the party stood in council elections across the North and won 59 seats. Sinn Féin had become a political force to be reckoned with.

The role of Sinn Féin's elected representatives grew in importance and Sinn Féin was developing party structures in each district. Increasingly, IRA personnel were being used to help in electioneering and the numbers engaged in operations began to fall, as did the number of operations themselves. Involvement in elections was yet another distraction for IRA volunteers like Gerry Bradley from what they saw as their main priority: fighting the British, a task that was becoming ever more challenging.

By the early 1980s, the British army was concentrating on intelligence as the primary means of tackling the IRA: surveillance, databases, electronic technology, recruiting double-agents, developing undercover work, as opposed to the crude house-to-house searching and screening of the male population of republican districts, the old 1970s processes that had antagonised the whole

Catholic community. The old procedures revealed that the British army had a dearth of what they called 'actionable intelligence'. In its 2006 analysis of the campaign in Northern Ireland, the army admits that, 'Without actionable intelligence of any appreciable quality or quantity, the security forces' main offensive option was to search occupied houses, usually conducted on the basis of low-grade tip-offs.'

By 1980, one in eight soldiers was directly involved in intelligence activity of some kind. The results were obvious and effective. The army searched 21,000 buildings in 1977. By the early eighties the numbers searched averaged 4,000 a year. By 1983 it was 1,500. They no longer needed speculative searching. By the end of the 1980s the IRA went for a period of two years without being able to detonate a single bomb in Belfast city centre. The army's analysis concludes that the importance of intelligence 'is hard to understate. The insurgency could not have been broken, and the terrorist structure could not have been engaged and finally driven into politics without the intelligence organisations and processes that were developed.'

Other refinements also made the work of the IRA difficult. The British army had learnt, to its cost, the shortcomings of repetitive foot-patrolling in the same streets at the same time, one man behind the other – a 'duck patrol' as it was known. First, they modified this approach to parallel patrolling so that an attack on one patrol would still leave the parallel one free to retaliate. By the 1980s, patrolling had become enormously more sophisticated. The army used what they called 'multiples' – half a platoon divided into teams who patrolled in an unpredictable fashion, each team supporting the others, criss-crossing streets.

For most of the 1970s, British army radios did not work in built-up areas, so patrols could not communicate. By the 1980s, with radios that enabled constant communication, patrol teams knew exactly where all the others were. It was practically impossible for an IRA gunman to fire his weapon and get away because of the likelihood of meeting a team of soldiers on his 'run back'.

In Belfast, the IRA never successfully developed the skill of sniping. Gerry Bradley says that, as far as he knows, no one in the Belfast IRA could use a telescopic sight. The British army's report says there was only one IRA man, a south Armagh operator, who could snipe in the proper sense of the word – that is, being able to hit a target from a range greater than 300 metres. In the case of the south Armagh man, he was successful on one occasion from 850 metres. In Belfast, occasionally, individuals like Davy Mackie, mentioned earlier, were successful with aimed shots at short range, say thirty to fifty metres. But the usual approach was to blaze away at close range, then run. The technique of 'multiples' patrolling effectively ended this kind of shoot-and-run tactic.

Perhaps even more damaging to IRA morale than British intelligence advances was the emergence in 1981 of supergrasses, the first of whom was Christopher Black, from the Bone district, close to Ardoyne. His evidence, in effect, resulted in virtually every member of the IRA in Ardoyne, who was not already in jail, being arrested. As well as supergrasses, it is now also known that by 1980

British intelligence and RUC Special Branch had several highly placed informers in the Belfast IRA, whose information regularly managed to stymie operations.

The improved tactics of the British army and police, allied with the decisive switch towards politics, began to change the direction of the whole republican movement. IRA operations that went 'wrong' began to cause embarrassment. For example, a week before Christmas 1983, a bomb exploded outside Harrods, the fashionable shop in Knightsbridge, London, killing three police and three civilians and injuring 75 others, many seriously. One of those killed was an American citizen. Several of the injured were people from mainland European countries, who were in London for Christmas shopping. Gerry Adams found himself having to try to explain the IRA's rationale to the world's press. He urged the IRA 'to be careful and careful again'.

The trouble was, of course, that the Harrods bomb had not gone 'wrong'. It had done its job in frightening off Christmas shoppers from central London, but it was a political and public relations disaster, impossible to justify. Local initiative, whether in Belfast or London, had the potential to derail political strategy. The logic was for more and more operations to be controlled, or at least sanctioned, by the IRA leadership in case they conflicted with Sinn Féin political aspirations.

Like most IRA men, Gerry Bradley was unconvinced by the growing importance of electoral politics in the republican movement. He couldn't believe that politics would lead anywhere except into the British system in the North. He interpreted any concession from the British as a sign of weakness, the result of the IRA campaign rather than of Sinn Féin's electoral successes. His attitude was confirmed by the official line from the top of the IRA in public and private, namely that the IRA campaign and political activity would go on in parallel – the 'Armalite and ballot box' strategy. The leadership had to sell this line to the rank and file because any suggestion of running down the military side of affairs before any discernible advance on the IRA's aims would not only have spread alarm and despondency; it would have caused a split. So volunteers were told the campaign was going to step up a gear.

What would Bradley have done differently? 'I know you need a political wing and it's important to get votes to endorse the IRA campaign, but, if there's a campaign, then you have to devote resources to it. From 1982 the campaign was being run down, I know that now. Over the years, all the resources were switched to the political side. I remember being furious when a Sinn Féin councillor told me Adams had said to him Sinn Féin workers were as important as volunteers.

'If it hadn't been for the IRA, the British would never have negotiated with Sinn Féin. It was the IRA who put Sinn Féin where it is. Instead of running down the campaign, I would have conducted it more strategically. If we were supposed to be destroying the North's economy and keeping it unstable, then do it. Go out and shoot investors, industrialists – stop people putting money in here.

'Take the war to England. I was always strongly in favour of that.

As they say, one bomb in London is worth a hundred here, and it's true. Look at Canary Wharf [February 1996] – that got faster results than a million votes. Also did more damage than a hundred bombs in Belfast. John Major didn't want that again. Shoot MPs. Exploding bombs here or killing the odd soldier didn't put the guy in Whitehall off his dinner. Blow up the Stock Exchange, the Bank of England, shoot a couple of MPs. Anybody who says that doesn't produce political results is lying. Look, why did the Brits talk to us in 1992 and 1993 when the England department [of the IRA] was blowing the City of London to bits? To get us to stop, that's why.

'I'd have kept the campaign and the political wing parallel. That's what the leadership was promising in 1981, Armalite and ballot box and all that. Didn't happen. "Conditioning" was the key word. The leadership "conditioned" people right through the 1980s. Got them ready to accept the next step, and the next step was always the IRA taking a step back.

'I believed them when they said the campaign was moving up a gear after the Libyan gear came in [1985-87]. I was ready to go out there and get myself killed. I feel so betrayed by what happened, the way it happened and the way they lied to us over the years. I was in jail after the ceasefire (which I agreed with because we were to get into negotiations with the Brits). There was to be no decommissioning. All that "not an ounce" business [reference to an IRA slogan "Not an ounce, not a bullet"]. In fact, they were waiting for the right moment to destroy all the gear and put the IRA out of business. If they'd kept the IRA strong, they'd have got a lot more out of the Brits than they settled for in 1998.'

From the outset, in 1982, Gerry Bradley spurned attempts to get him involved in the new focus on politics. One IRA member, Alex M., encouraged Bradley to get involved in community work in Unity. Sinn Féin and IRA members were taking over from community and voluntary workers on committees and tenant associations and community groups all over republican Belfast. Could Bradley do his bit?

Initially, Bradley gave it a go, but he soon pulled out. 'All I was doing was pushing out this woman, Jean Reilly, who loved her community work, who was brilliant at it. She loved the kids. She stood up for them. It was her life. She went everywhere on a bicycle, did all sorts of voluntary work. She was miles better at it than me. She knew what she was doing.' Besides, although Bradley reckoned taking a lead in community life was essential and did advance the republican cause, he certainly did not think that making a man like him chairman of a local community centre would produce any benefit.

Equally, Bradley kept out of the republican movement's increasingly powerful 'civil administration', as it was called. The civil administration was the branch of the republican movement that ran local districts. 'When the ASUs began operating at the end of 1973, they were "separated out" from rank-and-file IRA members who went to form the civil administration.' The civil administration was in full flow by 1976. The IRA ran it and continued to do so. The IRA members in it were those who did not want to operate.

They could be intelligence officers, even quartermasters, but not operators. Some people involved in it also had dual membership of Sinn Féin and the IRA, but 'you had to be in the army to play a part in the civil administration.'

Civil administration was a crucial component in Gerry Adams's reorganisation of the republican movement when he was released from jail in 1976. One of Adams's chief objections to the 1975 ceasefire was that, as he said in his book *Before the Dawn*, if you only have an army and no political party and you call a ceasefire, you have nothing. He believed it was essential to build up political consciousness in republican districts and develop a political movement before there was ever another ceasefire. The civil administration of the mid-1970s was the embryo of what became the Sinn Féin political machine in each republican locality in the eighties.

The whole concept had its origins in the way Sinn Féin took over the functions of the British administration in Ireland in 1919, establishing its own Sinn Féin courts, running its own postal service, setting up a rudimentary bank system through the republican loan scheme Michael Collins ran. In many parts of the country, from 1919 on, Ireland's underground Sinn Féin government, with its own ministries, generally acted as the elected government of the Irish people, right down to issuing items like driving licences. Operating in republican districts of the North from the 1970s, Sinn Féin tried as far as possible to copy this Sinn Féin strategy of 1919 and behave like an underground administration, controlling the daily activities of people in the districts they dominated.

They operated out of 'incident centres' that the British government had provided in republican districts during the 1975 ceasefire to encourage republicans to get into politics. Originally, incident centres were established to allow a direct line between the local IRA and the British army to report 'incidents' of ceasefire breaches, hence their name. Members of the civil administration quickly began to respond to general complaints from locals coming to the incident centres, which the British had equipped with telephones and telex machines (which, of course, were all bugged).

'Guys from the civil administration did the batterings etc.', that is to say, punishment beatings and shootings of people involved in 'anti-social behaviour' and criminal activity. Like other ASU members, Bradley took no part in any of that. 'ASU men tended to remain separate from the civil administration. If someone came to you and reported something, you would pass it on to one of the guys in the civil administration. Operators would have a kind of seniority in the district. People looked up to them.'

To place ASU's in context, they were the IRA's combat squads. By the mid-1980s, according to British intelligence, there were only about sixteen ASU's in the IRA, half a dozen based in the North, including three covering west and north Belfast. The battalion and company structures had gone. The ASU's carried out all the IRA's military activities. Each was made up of four to ten men and women. In Belfast, they were more flexible than those based south of the border, which tended to specialise either in bombing or in shooting. In Belfast, the two or three ASU's had expertise in both bombing and shooting. If, as Martin McGuinness said in 1985, the IRA was 'the cutting edge' of the struggle, the ASU's were the IRA's sharp point. The rest of the IRA serviced them and, as the eighties wore on, increasingly the bulk of IRA members were not involved in shooting or bombing but were being sucked into the civil administration, then into politics.

'Even by the time of the hunger strikes in 1981, the IRA was running whole areas and dealing with all kinds of stuff, from complaints about the milkman to marriage guidance, to aggravated burglary. People went to the cops about car accidents because you had to, for the insurance, and for broken windows to the Housing Executive. Otherwise, the IRA dealt with everything. The only crime people went to the police about was paedophiles – even then, the civil administration often got to the main actor first.'

By the mid-1980s, the civil administration was the dominant element in the republican organisation in each district. It had a manifold role. Apart from dealing with complaints and acting as a local police force, its members serviced IRA squads operating in the district. Bradley says the administration could produce a weapons dump, materiel, a safe house, a call house. They gathered intelligence, liaised with IRA squads, kept them informed about what was happening with British army units and RUC in the district. The administration also tried to provide work for men and women coming out of jail, usually in one of the many community endeavours the IRA ran in each local area: community centres, bars, clubs, taxis, building sites.

Bradley was conscious that 'in the 1980s all the resources were going to politics and elections, community groups, campaigning, organising for election day. The war was being run down. I can see that now. There had been rumours as early as 1983 that Adams was running the war down. I asked about the rumours, but the men I asked, well up in the 'RA, denied it, said there was more gear coming in. Probably they were organising the Libyan stuff then.' That was the official line, which Bradley accepted.

Even members of ASUs, like Bradley, were recruited to help out at election time. He remembers his first election, the 1985 council elections. The Sinn Féin candidate for the Unity Flats district was Fitz, who had been OC in Long Kesh in the seventies. Unity did not have enough voters to form a ward of Belfast city council, so was part of Court ward, a predominantly loyalist electoral district, stretching up the Shankill. The loyalist candidate in the area at the time was George Seawright, a Scot from Glasgow living in Belfast, a blindly bigoted extremist who had thrown in his lot with the DUP. He was actually a member of the UVF, a fact not acknowledged until 2003. At the election count, Bradley noticed him walking about in the company of John Bingham, the UVF boss in north Belfast.

Bradley was one of Fitz's election agents. He did not have much of a clue about the details of an election count. He was an interested observer. What he does recall is that he had 'never felt hatred like it coming from the counters' towards the Sinn Féin election workers. Meanwhile, he and his IRA colleagues, drafted in as Sinn Féin election workers, were more interested in busily trying to gather as much intelligence as they could about the people around Seawright who might be targeted as UVF men and about the interior of the City Hall, with a view to finding the best locations for explosives.

As a French polisher, he also took a professional interest in some of the magnificent woodwork and marble in City Hall. When he remarked on the marble walls to Alex Maskey, Sinn Féin's first councillor in Belfast since 1920, Maskey joked, 'Don't worry, when we take over here we'll soon have it covered with beauty-board', a reference to the cheap particle-board wood-effect sheeting that covered uneven, damp walls in many republican drinking clubs in Belfast. In 1985, it seemed a preposterous suggestion that Sinn Féin would ever be in a position to control Belfast City Hall. Seventeen years later, Maskey would become the first Sinn Féin lord mayor of Belfast.

The switch to IRA men helping out Sinn Féin's electoral endeavours and the increased power and influence of the civil administration in the mid-1980s, was a surprise to many veteran IRA men. Bradley recalls the astonishment of Martin Meehan, just out of jail in 1985 for his third or fourth time. Meehan was having a 'buster' (Belfast IRA rhyming slang for a meeting, as in 'a Buster Keaton') in Highbury Gardens in Ardoyne. Bradley says, 'He didn't know who they all were and what was going on. He thought it was an IRA buster he was running, which it was, and he was all for planning ops, getting things moving. He was just out of jail and here he was, ready to take the lead in ops at his age [he was forty]. It didn't work like that any more. I told him some of the guys at this buster didn't operate. He couldn't believe it. Meehan says, "Are youse all in the IRA?" They nodded. He says, "Is there anyone here doesn't want to operate? Anybody doesn't want to operate, out, to fuck."'

It then had to be explained to Meehan that people could now join the IRA and pick their briefs. He would not accept that either. He couldn't imagine how someone could join the IRA and decide he was going to be, say, an intelligence officer. He was bewildered. It was the IRA, but not as Martin Meehan, who had been operating since 1969, knew it. He thought that with all these men there should be a lot more action. He did not realise that action was now down to the ASU squads alone. Bradley took basically the same view as Meehan. He kept the civil administration at arm's length, as much as he could, not able to foresee that within a decade it would be people who started off their IRA careers in the civil administration who would be telling the IRA operators what to do.

The obstacles that electoral politics placed in the way was only one dimension of the difficulties IRA operators faced. When Bradley was well enough to begin operating again in the mid-1980s, he says he noticed how much tighter security was, how much more difficult it was to carry out operations. Bradley came to run an ASU in north Belfast, and was joined by Larry Marley, who had been released from jail in 1985 after serving almost ten years. Marley was one of the brains behind the mass IRA jail-break from the Maze prison in 1983, but took no part in the break-out himself because his release date was so close. Running operations in north Belfast, Bradley and Marley were really up against it. They were faced with the noticeable improvement in the technology the British had at their disposal, their new tactics and also the constant threat from informers.

Aerial supremacy was the principal advantage the British had. 'The chopper destroyed us. If the chopper was up, you weren't allowed to move out of a house: army orders. You stayed in whatever house you were in. Ops were cancelled regularly because of it. They could read your newspaper over your shoulder from the chopper. I once watched the chopper following a guy heading through the New Lodge district to work on a building site, where he was to meet me. We moved to another house in the site. It followed us. Then it hovered there. If the chopper spots one major player in the wrong place, that's it, an op is ruined. There were two choppers up in Belfast permanently. They were everywhere in south Armagh. That's why McGack [McGahey] took risks to get Redeyes.'

He cites the example of a 'big op' with a 500kg bomb, involving a large team, maybe ten men, including himself. The bomb was destined for the Europa hotel, always a prestige target. 'The Brits have no idea how many times the Europa was a target – for its symbolism. It was hit a few times, right enough, but the aim was to bring it down. That bomb would have done it. From BB's [Belfast Brigade] point of view it was the only thing not wrecked in Belfast. Loads of ops on the Europa had to be cancelled.' He reckons the chopper spotted one member of the team in the wrong place and was able to track the progress of the 500kg bomb. It was stopped at Koram Ring in Andersonstown and the men transporting it were arrested.

'All the players were marked by the mid-eighties. The Brits noted where they were seen, where they were coming from and where they were going. The Brits in the street were no longer stopping the ordinary citizen, just the 'RA. It doesn't mean they left the civilian population alone. They weren't still doing screening and so on. It wasn't like in the seventies when they were "gripping" everyone all the time. Then you could be gripped eight or ten times in a couple of months. By the mid-eighties they would let a dozen guys walk past, but stop me or another 'RA man. They arrested you for seven days. They targeted individuals. You couldn't get into town. If you did, you'd be stopped in town. The 'RA took to using taxis to ferry men around. The Brits homed in on them immediately. They knew the firms. If they spotted a taxi in the wrong place, they'd stop it: "What's a north Belfast taxi doing running round west Belfast?"

'The technology was amazing. We tried to explain it to new volunteers, but it was hard to convince them. They thought the Brits had to have men with binoculars hiding in a building. They wouldn't believe video cameras could run for days. Yet the IRA had brilliant technology too, so if we had it why wouldn't they have it? The timer on the Brighton bomb [in 1984] ran for weeks. Electronics were coming in big time. We had to talk in bathrooms with the water running. We maybe didn't speak at all, but passed notes.

We always checked weapons looking for bugs, see if the stock showed signs of being recently removed. You never knew what stuff was in the watch-towers, so you took no chances.'

The watchtowers on high vantage points dominated republican districts. They bristled with aerials, directional microphones, powerful Super-Nikon binoculars, CCTV cameras with huge zoom lenses. Virtually all movement could be monitored. 'The stuff on top of Oldpark barracks meant we could only operate out of the three streets in Ardoyne that weren't covered from Oldpark. The Brits knew that and kept patrols in those streets.

'Brompton Park [in Ardoyne] was favourite for ops. You could work from the back of the houses where you couldn't be seen from Oldpark, run a wire from the house under a car parked at the front, and out to a bomb. The problem was that because they could watch the front of the houses from Oldpark, there weren't too many Brit patrols coming down the street to hit with a bomb.

'One time, two of us – me and a woman – took over a house in Brompton. I hated house take-overs because you only annoyed the people and gave grief, lost supporters. We were to run out a wire at night and wait for the morning. The guy in the house was huge, a monster, bigger than both of us together, but he didn't cause any upset. He was a lorry driver and he kept moaning about his lorry in the docks. He said it was blocking in all the other lorries and if he didn't move it first thing in the morning the owner would be up at the door, raising hell. He went on and on about that. Nothing we could do about that, though. Still, we worried all night. What were we gonna do if the guy came up and who else knew he was coming up?'

Bradley and a local Explosives Officer, called ET, ran their wire out from the kitchen, drilled a hole in the architrave of the front door and led the wire out to a car that was parked with its boot facing the street. The bomb was in the boot and designed to explode outwards towards the British army patrol. The firing point was in the kitchen to enable Bradley and the woman to escape out of the back of the house.

Bradley says: 'The big guy was telling the truth. First thing in the morning there's a ring at the door. The big driver answered it. The guy comes in: "What's happening? That lorry has to be moved," and so on. We had the balaclavas on, and the guns, and said: "IRA. This is an operation." What do you think? Your man, the boss, is from south Armagh. He changed straight away. "Brilliant," says he. "What's gonna happen? Is it a bomb? Is it for the Brits?" And all that sort of stuff. He wanted to wait to see what happened. He forgot all about the lorry blocking the docks. Anyway, in the end the op was called off. Damp squib.'

It was typical of so many occasions when elaborate preparations came to nothing.

'There was a sangar on Templar House [in the New Lodge]. That one did so much damage. You could only walk up the left side of Spamount Street and a couple of other streets. Dozens of ops had to be called off because of it. They could watch the whole district. The Brits once shot a guy, Crawford, working on the roof of the

Felons' Club, with an air rifle from that sangar on Templar, just as a demo. Between the chopper and the towers, maybe 80 percent of ops had to be called off, maybe more. The 'RA never gave the Brits credit for this sort of thing. When something went wrong, it was always because of touts. It wasn't, but there were plenty of touts too – not just big-time informers, £5 touts. They just gave the Brits low-level stuff, anything they saw or heard. A lot of them were straight-out criminals – car thieves, robbers, drug pushers.'

Nevertheless, there were many informers and many worked undiscovered at a high level in the IRA, dramatically increasing the odds against successful operations. The IRA, in all its incarnations from 1919 to the present day, had always been plagued by informers, and members were always on their guard against the prospect of being betrayed. But IRA men never seemed to expect someone fully active in the movement to be guilty, even though the British would be most likely to target a person as active and as close to the centre of affairs as possible. So it was always a shock when an operator was exposed, especially a close comrade.

Being fingered by Charlie McKiernan in 1981 had been an awful psychological shock for Bradley, but McKiernan's information was limited in scope: one squad, one operation. There had been other instances, however, which had not impinged on Bradley's personal freedom but had a major impact on the whole republican movement in Belfast. One was the case of Peter Valente.

Valente was an IRA member from Stanhope Drive in Unity Flats. In 1980 Bradley was approached by a north Belfast man, who'd had an assignation with a married woman in a country hotel. While having a meal with the woman, this man saw Valente, whom he knew, with a policeman he recognised. Valente spotted the north Belfast man and came over to talk to him. He told him he was casing the hotel for an IRA bombing operation. Valente did not know the man had also recognised his companion as a policeman. Gerry Bradley promptly passed on this information to Paddy McManus, a veteran IRA man from the New Lodge. 'The next thing I heard, Valente was lifted and whacked. He told his interrogators, "I'm not a tout; I'm a British agent." When they came to take him out to be shot, he said, "OK, come on, let's go."'

The extent of Valente's betrayal was hugely shocking and embarrassing for the IRA in Belfast. Valente came from a republican family. He had a close relative 'on the blanket' at the time. To try to avoid humiliating the family and revealing what Valente had done, the IRA dumped the body in the loyalist Highfield estate and, unusually, issued a false statement praising Valente's work for the H-block campaign and blaming the UDA for the killing, a statement immediately repudiated by the RUC.

Like all such killings of informers, the shooting of Valente sent ripples through the IRA in Belfast. What had he told the Special Branch? What did they know? Also, under interrogation by the IRA's Internal Security, he had apparently implicated other IRA men and republican supporters as informers. Did he? Were they? It is now known that the IRA's internal security team was hopelessly compromised, probably from as early as 1979. What information, if any, did Valente really give them? Was the 'information' Valente is alleged to have given to internal security accurate, or invented to cause turmoil among the IRA's Belfast Brigade? If so, it certainly seems to have succeeded, because the IRA shot at least three others on foot of information extracted from Valente. Were they informers? Who knows the truth except RUC Special Branch and British intelligence?

If Valente's exposure sent shock waves through the Belfast Brigade, the impact of the first supergrass, Christopher Black, caused an earthquake in 1981. Black, from the Bone, had been a minor IRA operator, but knew the ins and outs of the IRA in Ardoyne and the Bone intimately. In his evidence he implicated over forty people, many of whom were only auxiliaries, republican supporters or simply people who had let their houses be used for meetings. Most of them were charged. Some spent two years remanded in custody. Eventually, in 1983, twenty-two people were convicted of IRA-related offences and sentenced to a combined total of over four thousand years in jail. In the end, eighteen of them had their convictions overturned on appeal in 1986. It was a long, destructive saga for the IRA.

Despite the acquittals, says Bradley, 'Black wiped out Ardoyne and the Bone. The Crum [Crumlin Road jail] was bunged: three in a cell for a while. He had a terrible domino effect too. People stopped leaving their doors open. They were scared to help. They had seen people charged for stupid little things. They couldn't trust the IRA any more. Black had an effect on morale and confidence for years. There was nobody in Ardoyne by 1986. That's why me and Marley were running the squad then.'

Marley was too much of a 'red light' to be out on operations, having just emerged from jail. If caught again, he was looking at a colossal sentence. Besides, he was forty-one, too old to be charging about the streets. However, he was an able and careful organiser and planner; those were his strengths. Bradley looked after the sharp end of things – shooting and bombing. He had known most of the ASU members in different capacities for years and trusted them. Usually he operated with four others: Ruby Davison, 'Bootser', Paddy McD and Paddy Murray, whom he did not know personally.

Bradley was thirty-two at this stage, as fully recovered as he ever would be from his gunshot wounds, fit and active and keen as ever. For the most part, 'We tried to carry out "snipes" in the Markets or in Newington or the New Lodge, the occasional bomb, but it was getting more and more difficult. Everything had to be okayed by brigade. We were still up for any big op we could manage, but the danger of civilian casualties stopped so many or Brigade turned them down with no reason.

'One plan was to have a go with one of the 50–50 [half-inch] heavy machine guns that came from Libya.' These were Russian weapons known as DshK (nicknamed 'Dushka', 'Sweetie' or 'Dearie' in Russian), used as anti-aircraft weapons by the Vietcong and easily capable of bringing down a helicopter. 'They were real brutes. They needed four men to operate them if you hadn't the wheels. We thought of firing from a house and even from the back of a van or lorry. The front two men had to wear bullet-proof vests, because if the Brits fired back they were going to get hit. They couldn't run anywhere or take cover.

'One of the squad had the idea to drive in a van in front of an army Land Rover, open the back doors and let fly. The fire power was devastating. You'd kill the driver and passenger and the bullets would go through to the back of the Land Rover and hit the rest of the crew. Only snag was any rounds that missed the Land Rover or went through it would travel on and could kill people a mile away. Three ops with the 50–50 were called off.'

Needless to say, neither that, nor any similar operation in Belfast, got off the ground. So many operations were being cancelled or stymied, there was increasing anxiety to have a success. It smacked of desperation.

As well as planning operations, abortive in most cases, Bradley also built up contacts for intelligence: 'People in dental records, the Housing Executive, the post office – you name it. It all went up to brigade. For an op, you get as many connections as possible. The BBIO [Belfast Brigade intelligence officer] has most links over Belfast and can see the whole picture. All info goes to Brigade and it's sifted; nothing thrown away. It was kept in dumps, like weapons. The Brigade double O [Operations Officer] could okay an op or turn it down, sometimes because of intelligence that had come in that you never know about.'

Sometimes, however, it did not require the resources of Brigade or an extensive intelligence exercise to deduce that something was wrong. In 1986, Bradley began to realise that the informer virus had infected the small Belfast squads. First, there were warning signs. A blast bomb thrown at an RUC Land Rover in the Short Strand exploded, but the explosion did not penetrate the armour. Some time later, IRA intelligence heard that a community worker talking to an RUC man about the incident had said it was a lucky escape. 'Lucky?' said the policeman. 'No, the Land Rover that day was a "hard-skinned" vehicle.' Incredibly, the policeman added, 'We were expecting it.' How did the police know there was going to be an attack that day?

Secondly, in the course of one of Bradley's regular visits to Castlereagh, the police had either stupidly or deliberately mentioned operations that had not come off or had been at the planning stage. When he got out of Castlereagh and was being debriefed in Jamaica Street in Ardoyne, Bradley said to his debriefer, Freddie Scapaticci: 'Something's going on. How do they know about ops that never happened? I'm not doing any more until it's sorted out.' Scapaticci said: 'Look, there's a big inquiry going on.' Was *that* exactly what Special Branch wanted? Sowing doubts in activists' minds?

By this time Scapaticci ran the IRA's fearsome Internal Security, in Belfast, and was number two overall in Internal Security to John Joe Magee, an ex-Royal Marine and former member of the Royal Navy's élite Special Boat Squadron. Martin Meehan once said, 'IRA volunteers are more scared of IRA security than they are of Brit security forces.' And with good reason. Once 'arrested' on suspicion by Internal Security, an IRA member could anticipate at least a beating, perhaps brutal torture if there was any evidence to confirm Internal Security's suspicions, and sometimes even if there was not, and ultimately a bullet in the head.

Bradley says the Internal Security squad based in Belfast were 'complete incompetents, drunks, wasters. Sometimes people confuse them with the "Nutting Squad". They wouldn't have had the balls. They did the beatings, torturing, but not the killing. They spent their days in the pub at the bottom of Clonard Street. They did their interrogations in a house near the pub so they didn't have to walk too far.'

Obviously the 'big inquiry' extended beyond the Belfast Internal Security team, because the first member of Bradley's squad lifted as part of their 'big inquiry' was Paddy McD. 'McD had been sent to south Armagh to collect "blowy stuff" [explosives]. It was a ploy. Once there, McD was arrested, zipped up in a sleeping bag and beaten black and blue, but he had nothing to tell. He was innocent. The guys who beat him up were a disgrace. They stole his necklace and wedding ring.'

When he got back to Belfast, a very thankful man but very sore, he told Bradley, who was furious. He regarded it as a personal sleight that a member of the squad had been lifted. He raised a stink about the whole incident, and the theft of the jewellery. There was an IRA Court of Inquiry, in which Brendan 'Darkie' Hughes played a role, and the culprits were 'held accountable', whatever that means.

Internal Security was working its way through the whole squad. 'They sickened people, lifting totally innocent guys. Was that deliberate?' They arrested Bradley and took him to the house near their pub. He was tied up in a darkened room. 'I reared up at them because I could smell they had drink on them while they were doing interrogations.' He knew a couple of them from being in a squad with them in the seventies. 'They were just drunks by now. Incompetents. They didn't know what they were doing half the time. Scap and his lot hadn't been on ops for years. They knew nothing. I told them I was expecting them. They said, "How did you know?" I said Paddy McD told me. "Oh", they said, "he wasn't supposed to tell anyone!" Pathetic.'

The whole performance of arresting and questioning all the squad was probably for show. As a British agent, Scapaticci should have known who the culprit guilty of passing information about the attack on the RUC Land Rover in the Short Strand was: Paddy Murray. Did the British tell Scapaticci it was Murray or did they sacrifice Murray, turn a blind eye to his fate? Was it to preserve Scapaticci, or someone else?

'Me and Paddy McD were organising to whack a peeler in the Short Strand. A peeler opened the barrier at Mountpottinger barracks every day. We were going to use a .303. We had a house overlooking where he would be. Paddy Murray was from the Short Strand, Beechfield Street. He was the main organiser. I was going to do the shoot. You couldn't miss. The house we had was so close you could have thrown the rifle out the window and hit him. I trained in Maysfield leisure centre [beside the Markets – a mile away] every day, so I'd a reason for being there. The plan was I'd be in my training gear. I'd whack the peeler, drop the weapon, and the two of us come out of the house, like, jogging, run over the bridge to Maysfield, get a shower, get changed and away.

'Paddy Murray kept pushing, pushing for the op, but Marley was not supplying the .303, even though we'd hundreds of .303s. In fact, Marley was linked up with the Belfast OC. They knew someone was informing, but weren't sure who. Marley wasn't about to supply the .303 to set the shooting in train for the whole squad to get lifted if the op had been given away.

'Internal Security told Paddy Murray to come over. He arrives in the evening at the appointed time. He's blindfolded, tied up. They have Ruby Davison, another guy on the squad, tied up in the next room. "Right, Paddy, we know you're at it." "I figured youse did," says Paddy. "Who did you tell you were coming here?" they asked him. "I phoned my handler," he said.

'Panic. There's a scattering match. They ran in to the next room, got Ruby – can you believe this? – told Ruby, "Bring him round to this [named] house." Ruby walks Paddy round to the house. No blindfold now. Not tied up. Now can you believe this? Internal Security know he's a Brit agent. They know he's told his handler. Yet they brought him to another safe house. No weapons, no security. Is he carrying a homer [electronic homing device]? Ruby walks him two streets away. Later he asks, "Why didn't Murray run?"'

Now the real interrogation began. 'The reason Murray kept

pushing for the Short Strand op was that the SAS were waiting. Three times the SAS were waiting, because I would say, for example, "We're gonna do it on Tuesday morning", but no .303 came. He had the SAS waiting to kill me and McD. That's what he told Internal Security. Murray had also taken dets [detonators] out of bombs, prevented them exploding. He was handing his gear to the Brits, who jarked it. All because a few years before he got caught with a few rounds going over the bridge to the Short Strand and wouldn't do his time. He'd also got cash. The money and dets were found when the IRA raided his house.'

On 15 August 1986, Paddy Murray was shot dead in an alley off Dunmore Street in the Clonard district. According to the IRA, Murray had received £10,000 from RUC Special Branch in the eight years he had been informing since his arrest for possession of ammunition in 1978.

'Murray was a bricklayer. He made brilliant dumps. Once that year, 1986, we had a ten-pound gas canister full of gelly [gelignite]. We had sealed it with Isopon [a car repair kit that congeals with metal] and fused it. Murray had built it into a chimney breast, so you wouldn't notice. He made dumps like that. As soon as his body was found, the cops immediately did every dump Paddy Murray had. He had shown the cops them all.

'When the body was found, Ruby rang me up and said, "It's Paddy." I was walking through Smithfield later that day and met a girl, Marie, who had a dump he had made in her house. I told her to expect the cops. By the time she got home they were there, wrecking the place. In other words they knew every single place where the squad's gear was. They could watch who was coming to get it and they'd jarked all the weapons in the dumps. I was so shocked by Murray that I went on the drink for three days.

'The Brits sacrificed him. They knew he was going to Internal Security. He told them – but he'd served his purpose. They let him die, I believe, to protect somebody else: Scap, Magee? Who knows? Why did he not run? I think he was so embarrassed and ashamed by what he'd done over the years he wanted to be killed. Anyway, where was he running to?'

One who was not sacrificed was Eamon 'Budgie' Loughry. Years before, Loughry had been adjutant of G company in Unity, and was shot and wounded by marines in 1972. By the eighties, Loughry was living in the Newington district off the Antrim Road. 'He was a painter and decorator and ran a small business with a squad of men. However, he got government contracts. You needed clearance for that. How did he get clearance with his background, when people couldn't get clearance for work when they'd never done anything and were only related to republicans? How did the 'RA not cop on?'

Loughry was a useful contact who could keep stuff and get houses. Bradley says, 'He was well positioned to do big damage.' Bradley suspects Loughry sabotaged a lot of operations. I was told they reckon that Loughry cut the command wire of a bomb on at least one occasion.

Bradley's personal experience of Loughry had made him very

suspicious. 'One op was to whack two peelers who were on the beat on the Limestone Road. Me and a guy called Gary were going to walk up behind them and, Bang! Bang! I was told to link in with Loughry who was organising the back-up. I didn't like it. I told the double O I didn't want to deal with him because he wasn't trusted right back to the seventies; but he lived in Newington off the Limestone, and so had local knowledge, so the double O said we had to.

'Loughry was supposed to be organising the run back and houses and stuff. I said to him, "You know you're going to get a seven-dayer [seven days in Castlereagh] after this?" Loughry said, "So what?" Very suspicious. He didn't care. He didn't make any preparations for being lifted and you needed to if two peelers were whacked. You were gonna get a battering and a real hard time.

'A short time after Paddy Murray was killed, Larry Marley asked Loughry to go down to south Armagh for a genuine reason, but obviously Loughry thought he was for the high jump – south Armagh Internal Security, like Paddy McD. He blew. Vanished. The removal van was at his house in Newington and the whole kit and caboodle was away. He was wrong. It wasn't Internal Security. It was just Marley wanting a bit of gear moved, but Loughry thought he'd been rumbled and it flushed him out.'

In April 1987, after Loughry's flight, the UVF shot Larry Marley dead in his house in Ardoyne. Marley knew his life was in danger and always took elaborate precautions, including not opening his front door unless he knew who was there. There was a special routine, in the absence of which Marley would not even come to the door. For some years, it was generally believed in the Belfast IRA that Loughry had given away to the police the secret knock and password that brought Marley to his front door, and that the police gave it to the UVF. When Marley came up to the door, the UVF gunman opened fire through the door's panelling and killed him. After revelations in 2007 and 2008 about several other Belfast IRA men, people are now not so sure it was Loughry who gave away Marley's security procedures. There is at least one other leading candidate.

In view of the repeated failures of Internal Security in the eighties – their inability to clear out informers from the Belfast Brigade, to prevent operations being compromised and so on – it is amazing that at no stage was there any review of this group by the IRA leadership. Obviously, Bradley was not the only person who knew they spent their days sitting in a bar on the Falls Road and that they were more often than not the worse for wear.

Even more staggering, in the context of the continual failures of Internal Security, is that after a new OC was appointed in Belfast Brigade in the mid-eighties, and after Paddy Murray was outed, all operations in Belfast had first to be cleared by Internal Security, according to Bradley. Bradley was outraged. He had no respect for the men on the squad. In fact, he despised some of them. It had been years since any of them had been on an operation, and he felt they had no idea about operations. Certainly, the man in charge, Freddie Scapaticci, had not fired a shot at a policeman or soldier since the early seventies, if then.

It is now known, of course, that Scapaticci had been a British agent since at least 1979, and perhaps earlier. By requiring all Belfast operations to be vetted by Internal Security, the OC was unwittingly providing British intelligence with knowledge of all IRA plans in Belfast. Therefore, from about 1986 until Scapaticci fell under IRA suspicion in 1991, British intelligence was, to all intents and purposes, deciding which IRA operations to allow to run in Belfast and which to block. Little wonder there was almost no successful operation of significance by the Belfast Brigade in those years.

It is true that policemen and soldiers continued to be shot and killed, and that the occasional bomb exploded, causing death and injury, in those years. However, major set-piece operations had a nasty habit of going wrong or being disrupted by undercover British army units like 14th Intelligence, the FRU (Force Research Unit) or the SAS. For example, in June 1988, the IRA mounted a gun-and-rocket attack on North Queen Street joint RUC/army barracks. They travelled in a stolen Volvo, selected because it had a sunroof that could be opened to allow a man to stand up through it with an RPG-7 rocket launcher. One, a veteran north Belfast operator and former G company member, fired the missile at the fortified sangar at the entrance to the barracks. Other squad members in the car simultaneously opened fire.

The security forces had been forewarned. An SAS squad had taken up position inside the barracks, awaiting the IRA squad. They probably even knew which car to expect. As the IRA attack began, the SAS opened up with withering automatic fire from a variety of weapons, including a belt-fed heavy machine gun, despite being in a heavily built-up urban district. The soldiers admitted firing eighty shots, but witnesses claimed it was a lot more. Amazingly, the IRA squad all escaped after abandoning their car. Unfortunately, some of the army's high velocity bullets travelled through the IRA's vehicle and hit a passing taxi, wounding the driver, who died of a coronary three days later. It was a classic SAS ambush, which, on that occasion, went wrong.

IRA operations, such as the North Queen Street attack, had become a rarity in Belfast. More often, operations had to called off. Time and again, bombs being transported into the city were intercepted by police and army just after they left Andersonstown or Ardoyne. Indeed, Belfast Brigade's most successful ploy during this period was repeatedly to bring Belfast to a standstill during the rush hour, with hoax bombs and bogus warning phone calls.

By the end of the eighties, Gerry Bradley was increasingly frustrated by the lack of impetus in the IRA in Belfast. He had a couple of rows at 'busters' with OC Belfast. He was amazed, on one occasion, to hear the OC saying that the British knew he was OC Belfast and liked him being OC because they knew the sort of guy he was, and that he wouldn't do anything crazy. According to Bradley, he said, 'They prefer me to the likes of'... and he looked around the room ... 'Gary, there. He's a complete lunatic and so unpredictable you wouldn't know what he'd do.' Bradley says, 'Gary didn't see the significance of it and he was nodding, saying, "Yeah, I'd be setting up ops all the time and bombing such and such."' Bradley thought to himself: Does the OC hear what he's saying? Does he know what that means?

Bradley was also unhappy at the way the man had become OC Belfast, though he obviously did not know at the time that the manoeuvring was part of the leadership's wider scheme to switch emphasis from military to political. '"Chalk" Carmichael was OC in the early eighties, and the new man was in Long Kesh, but while still inside he was selecting his brigade staff. He knew he was going to be replacing Chalk when he came out. He was telling people not to report back to Chalk when they got out. That wasn't right. It broke all sorts of army orders. All the deals were done inside before the new man got out. It nearly split the army in Belfast. Ruby Davison played a big part in holding things together. He was brought to Gerry Adams by a senior republican called Kelly and told him what was going on and what had happened in the jail, but nothing was done about it.

'Chalk was pushed out of the way, along with Ivor Bell [in 1985]. I mean, Bell was a guy who'd been OC Belfast and on the army council. In the end, they were both expelled from the IRA because they wanted to up the ante. It was the same story everywhere. Gerry Adams had got his men round him in the seventies and placed them everywhere. The new OC would do exactly what he was told.

'Anyway, the number of ops was down as well because the pressure was on not to injure civilians: that was counter-productive.

The main danger was hurting our own people. You had to avoid that at all costs. Everything was being tightened. They worried about "international opinion", about "electoral considerations". You practically had to guarantee no one would be injured by mistake. Sinn Féin were taking over. The politicians were running everything. Guys were prepared to do anything, but the double O would just say, "No". The double O was being told to sit on potential civilian casualties.

'It was a matter of pride to get around all the technology the Brits had and still not hurt any civilian. Because of that, ops were scrubbed often. You always erred on the side of doubt.

'We planned loads of stuff that never got anywhere. There was an idea to blow up the main sewer in North Street [leading to the city centre] with a small bomb that would ignite the methane gas and cause a huge blast, but there was no way you'd avoid civilian casualties, even at night. In another plan, we had lift engineers in, looking at the lifts in Templar House [in the New Lodge] to blow up the army sangar on top that was giving us all the grief. We were thinking of any way to do it: attaching a bomb with a magnet to a lift with Brits going up in it; dropping a bomb on a lift going down with Brits in it. But you were gonna hurt people in the flats.

'One op at the corner of Clifton Street was going to be the "op of the century". During an Orange march, you always got stacks of peelers lined up in front of the screens in jeeps and standing around. There was going to be a 500lb bomb behind the wall there, with a command wire. We reckoned it was going to kill fifty police.

No civilian casualties there. An informer from the New Lodge gave it away. The Brits got him out to Canada, where he lives to this day.

'Some ops got nowhere because of a comedy of errors. I had a flat in Kinnaird Terrace, overlooking Girdwood barracks [the biggest British army barracks in Belfast]. You could see all over the barracks. I reckoned we could mortar the barracks. We needed photos to plan where to aim the mortars. I got Paddy McManus to take the pictures. It was a perfect op. Any explosions – inside the base. No civilians. Paddy came in with this camera with a huge lens and took the pictures from the flat. And I sent them to be developed in the right place. Got them back. Nothing. Paddy forgot to take the lens cap off.'

Of course, Gerry Bradley did not know in the late eighties that the peace process had already begun. For the June 1987 British general election, Sinn Féin had produced a manifesto entitled *A Scenario for Peace*. Gerry Adams was now talking about the armed struggle as 'a tactic'. Conceivably, tactics could change. Adams said he 'gave critical support to the IRA'. Sinn Féin also began a series of public talks with the SDLP in 1988, after which Gerry Adams continued to talk privately to the SDLP leader, John Hume, in a series of talks that would continue until 1993, when the pair produced what came to be called the 'Hume–Adams Document'. In this new climate, there was no place for the continuous, unrelenting campaign IRA operators like Gerry Bradley were advocating. The armed struggle to which Bradley had devoted his life was now being relegated to a mere tactic instead of being the IRA's *raison d'être*.

Instead of ordering operations as frequently as possible in the North of Ireland, the IRA leadership began to concentrate on 'spectaculars', as they called them – major bombs at prestige targets, especially in England. There was a conviction that 'one bomb in England is worth a hundred in Ireland' because casualties or damage in Belfast, no matter how serious, cost the British government no votes and cut no ice with a British public, long fed up with the endless violence. The IRA leadership decided to harness Bradley's appetite for action and well-developed military talents for purposes other than exclusively waging war on the British.

9

THE WHEEL OF FORTUNE

'I had asked to go to England. I wanted to go, wanted to finish what
my da had started [in 1939]. I wanted to do as much damage
as possible, and London was the place. I knew I would be caught
or killed if I went. Anyone going to England in a "coffin" for an op
knew they were getting caught or killed. Escaped prisoners
often went to England. If you escape you're going on active service.
You're not going to last long.'

External pressures from British counter-insurgency strategies and
internal pressures from political exigencies were combining, from
the mid-eighties onwards, to make IRA operations more difficult
to execute. By the 1990s, all these pressures of the eighties had
grown into serious constraints on those in the IRA keen to carry on
'the war'. On the security side, British army surveillance had taken
a leap forward: satellite surveillance, electronics, real-time heli-telly
from helicopters, bugging devices, covert video cameras disguised
as stones, tree stumps or fallen branches, and advances in comput-
ing and telecommunications were leaving the IRA's experts behind.

Increased undercover work by locally recruited agents who had infiltrated the IRA, and by policemen and soldiers who operated in disguise in republican districts, made it difficult to know who to trust or where was safe. A significant number of men in key positions in Sinn Féin and the IRA, including men who acted as bodyguards to Gerry Adams – and even his driver – had been 'turned' by British intelligence in the mid-eighties. These men's role as agents was not revealed until twenty years later. As more and more information about highly placed informers became public in 2007 and 2008, Gerry Bradley would shake his head at each revelation and ask ruefully, 'How did we get anything done?' To top it all off, the number of IRA operators was drying up. 'There were plenty of volunteers joining the IRA who wanted to be intelligence officers or be in the civil administration, but not too many wanting to operate.'

For the leadership of the republican movement, politics were now the dominant consideration and politics had taken a remarkable turn by the end of the eighties. The events from 1989 to 1991, both in Britain with the demise of Thatcherism, and farther afield in the Soviet Union and eastern Europe, presented fundamental challenges to the IRA's concept of armed struggle, but also offered opportunities for a settlement with the British government that they had been angling for.

In Britain, Margaret Thatcher, the republican movement's nemesis, was cast aside by the Conservative party in November 1990. Thatcher had always refused to enter any kind of talks with republicans. Her unvarying line was that there would be no negotiations with terrorists. As soon as she was gone, the British Secretary of State in the North, Peter Brooke, began to respond to the feelers the IRA had been putting out. In an important speech in the month Thatcher was ousted, Brooke said Britain had 'no selfish strategic or economic interest' in the union. The British were well aware, from contacts with the Irish government and with John Hume, that Gerry Adams and Martin McGuinness wanted to bring the IRA campaign to an end. In 1991, British officials entered secret talks with the IRA in the persons of Martin McGuinness and Gerry Kelly.

Simultaneous with these developments in Britain, on the international scene there was the political and diplomatic earthquake that caused the fall of the Berlin Wall in 1989, the crumbling of the eastern bloc and finally, inevitably, the collapse of the Soviet Union in 1991. Commentators took this series of events to demonstrate conclusively the failure of Marxism as an ideology and a system of government. That failure automatically called into question the ideological basis for various struggles around the world. In many parts of Africa and Latin America, it was not simply an ideological matter. The USSR had been funding liberation movements and supplying them with weapons. That ceased. Almost immediately, these liberation movements had to consider their position. What relevance had their ideology now? What were the aims and aspirations of their armed struggles?

One of the movements affected was the struggle of the African National Council (ANC) in South Africa and its armed wing

Umkhonto We Sizwe. In the Middle East Yasser Arafat's Palestinian Liberation Organisation (PLO) had relied heavily on Soviet support in the United Nations. Both these movements quickly entered talks with their respective antagonists, in the case of the ANC, leading to success with the release of Nelson Mandela in 1990 and democratic elections in South Africa in 1994, in the case of the PLO, leading to the false dawn of the Oslo Accords in 1993, which were never implemented.

These seismic shocks struck Northern Ireland too. On the gable wall at the Falls Road end of Beechmount Avenue, in the heart of republican west Belfast, a brightly painted mural had, for many years, portrayed republican symbols alongside those of the PLO and ANC. A slogan read, 'PLO–ANC–IRA one struggle'. As Nelson Mandela and Yasser Arafat entered talks designed to bring their armed struggles to an end, where did that leave the IRA? They could not remain out on a limb. They would be left like political dinosaurs, mouthing the slogans of a defunct ideology. In truth, of course, the leadership had been looking for a way out since before the end of the Cold War in 1989. Quoting the example of the PLO and ANC, the IRA followed suit almost in exact parallel with those other movements with whom they had developed links over the years. Their contacts were especially close with the ANC, some of whose senior members, like Cyril Ramaphosa, visited Belfast a number of times before and after the IRA ceasefire in 1994 to encourage republicans to make the change and explain how best to go about it.

It is clear now that the IRA campaign was petering out from the end of the 1980s. It is true there was an increased emphasis on bombing and shooting in England, but IRA operations tailed off rapidly in Northern Ireland and most noticeably in Belfast. In 1990 the IRA carried out only four killings in Belfast, and in 1991, for the first time ever, loyalist killings outnumbered those carried out by republicans.

The leaders of the IRA had to keep their operators busy for a number of reasons: to keep them on board, to maintain the threatening posture of the IRA, and, perhaps the most important consideration, to prevent splits. For these reasons, the IRA continued to deny publicly and, indeed, privately to its volunteers that there was any prospect of a ceasefire. Successful major operations in England, including in 1990 the killing of Ian Gow MP, Mrs Thatcher's former parliamentary private secretary and one of her strongest supporters, helped reinforce that denial. These attacks in England, right up until 1993, also helped keep the British government on tenterhooks about whether or not there would be a ceasefire, despite all the talks behind the scenes.

Nevertheless, IRA operations in the North were fewer in number and more carefully selected and targeted. What the IRA needed most by the early 1990s, was money to become a major player in politics rather than an unrelenting campaign, which would inevitably produce embarrassing civilian casualties. After all, they had nearly thirty advice centres in republican districts across the North to run. Paying the rates alone for these premises required a formidable amount of money, before lighting, heating, telephone and stationery costs were taken into account.

At the beginning of the nineties, Bradley was dimly aware of the prospect of a ceasefire. He knew there were some kind of talks going on, but he believed the leadership 'spin' that there would be no ceasefire until unspecified IRA conditions were met. He remained completely wrapped up in the world of IRA operations – 'planned' operations might be a more accurate description because, from Bradley's account, by the early nineties the planning stage was often as far as they got, as so many operations fell apart or had to be aborted.

Trying to predict and outsmart British surveillance and electronics became an overriding concern towards the end of the IRA campaign (though little did IRA squads know that informers in the movement regularly cancelled out whatever success they achieved in overcoming surveillance). Electronic counter measures (ECM), which the British could deploy, superseded anything the IRA had at their disposal. During the eighties, IRA engineers had developed and improved their methods of detonating bombs by remote control. Instead of one radio pulse, which the British could easily block, the IRA had moved to two, then to three pulses on different frequencies.

The IRA were also using walkie-talkies. 'But the Brits were scanning the airwaves, jamming all transmissions in certain areas. When they detected a transmission, they knew we were about. We sometimes did dummy conversations to watch how the Brits reacted, see what their patrols did. You noticed soldiers on a patrol had a wee aerial sticking out of a backpack. That could jam transmissions and stop a booby-trap bomb going off. We were driven back to lines [command wires]. Then, of course, the chopper was up looking for lines, and if the chopper was up, the op had to be called off – army orders.'

One incident will illustrate the risks and frustrations. Bradley was in a squad that was almost captured in the Lower Ormeau Road, probably because British army ECM had picked up transmissions. Organising the operation involved the twenty best operators in Belfast, a gathering which surely must have attracted the attention of British intelligence and double agents alike. The plan was to detonate a massive van bomb on the Ormeau Embankment by remote control as British troops drove past. There would have been many casualties. The squad had to have a clear line of sight across the River Lagan, so they had taken over a house in the Lower Ormeau district, overlooking the river. Without a command wire, no one would know where the bomb had been detonated from. Operating from across the river should have made it easy for the squad to escape.

The British army regularly used the Embankment as a route to transport troops from barracks in east Belfast and Holywood to west Belfast. Hardly anyone walked along the Embankment, which curves along the Lagan between a loyalist district and the republican Lower Ormeau. Behind the Embankment lay the Ormeau Park, so there should be no civilian casualties. Two members of the squad parked the van containing the bomb directly across the Lagan from the house they had commandeered. It was a Belfast City Council Parks Department van and trailer, so it looked the part, sitting there beside the Ormeau Park. As the three members of the squad in the house with the transmitter for the detonator waited for a military vehicle to pass, they noticed the traffic along the Embankment dwindle to a trickle, then stop altogether. Something was wrong. Then a Ford Sierra drove along the Embankment at high speed: police. Bradley thinks they were photographing the van or at least taking as close a look as possible.

The squad decided to detonate the bomb even without a military target. The idea of exploding it was that, at least, they could close the Embankment and cause maximum disruption. The huge explosion would also destroy any forensic evidence they had overlooked. They pressed the button on their remote control, but nothing happened. 'Suddenly there was a banging on the front door and there was oul' Gerry Hanna from the Markets, shouting, "Get out, run for it, the Brits are on to youse."' In a helter-skelter rush, the squad members in the house, two men, one called 'wee' Gerard, and a woman, escaped, but it had been a very close call.

According to the *Belfast Telegraph* that night, the security forces had picked up transmissions that led them to suspect the parked van and trailer. It would not have taken long to check with Belfast Parks Department whether their van should have been there. The next stage would have been to trace any transmission from a house overlooking the river. However, the British would not necessarily have known the exact house and the IRA's lookouts spotted soldiers arriving to search the district. It was a lucky escape. Subsequent checks on the electronic equipment by IRA explosives officers confirmed everything was in working order. British ECM had apparently jammed the IRA's remote control.

On the other hand, perhaps the British had 'leaked' the story to the *Belfast Telegraph* that ECM had blown the operation whereas, in reality, undercover people had seen operators moving stuff or acting suspiciously? Or perhaps one of their highly placed informers had told them? Who can tell?

Operations were foiled repeatedly. The RUC chief constable in the early 1990s said the security forces were foiling four out of five IRA operations. Gerry Bradley says perhaps more, maybe nine out of ten. Security-force knowledge of IRA 'players', safe houses and the homes of IRA sympathisers required all movement by IRA operators to be circumspect. People had to watch if they were being followed, double back on themselves whether on foot or in a car, try not to be seen with another 'player'. At planning meetings, people passed notes rather than speaking, in case the venue was bugged.

Weapons dumps had to be more and more sophisticated and foolproof. 'The IRA progressed all the time. Hides and dumps got excellent. "Floats" now had to be concealed behind skirting boards, in the architraves of doors and windows. They had to be really good jobs and they were. One time in the New Lodge, the Brits "did" a house they knew gear was in, but they couldn't find it. They did it three times and still couldn't find it. Sealed dumps were in walls, chimney breasts, under solid floors in kitchens, that sort of place. You wrapped the weapons in waterproof stuff, then slid them into a pvc pipe with two sealers, one at each end, and put them in the dump. In the nineties, we always checked incoming weapons for "homers". We took the butts off and checked for sensors, though the Brits were more concerned about dets [detonators] than rifles by then. There wasn't that much sniping any more.

'Moving gear was another issue. We moved weapons under rubble or bricks, in between hollowed-out planks. We used Post Office vans. We used taxis, coalmen, milkmen. For moving the blowy stuff [explosives] you couldn't beat horseboxes. The Brits' sniffer dogs couldn't get past the smell of the horse. Masses of stuff was moved in those boxes – tons.'

By this stage of the campaign, the early 1990s, the speed of the peace process was quickening. The pace had accelerated with the departure of Mrs Thatcher in November 1990, but the IRA continued to use their armed campaign as a lever in their talks. The IRA had mastered the technique of making powerful, massive bombs, in excess of 500 kilograms, and they began to concentrate on detonating these large bombs in England to create 'spectaculars', as they called them. The explosives for these bombs, ammonium nitrate fertiliser and diesel, were mixed in south Armagh or just across the border in Cavan or Monaghan, and transported to England, where they were put together with a kilo of the plastic high-explosive Semtex as a booster, then fused. The organisation required for such operations was considerable.

'You had to have a lot of people even to get one bomb over to England. There would maybe have been about thirty people involved in the Brighton bomb in 1984. Pat [Magee] may have done the front job, but the op was put together by a lot of people he never met. One individual would have a brief to get something from A to B, somebody else from B to C. They wouldn't know what each other was doing, or who the other people were. In England, especially, you had to keep things tight.

'The people going to England were transported in what were called "coffins", boxes and packing chests that went in container lorries, and the "coffins" were packed in as cargo. They'd be dropped off at various points in England. It was very important to get transport to and from England organised. One of my jobs in the early 1990s was to get lorries that couldn't be suspected or traced back. Getting dependable drivers was key. It wasn't just carrying people and stuff to England. The drivers also brought in gear to the North, especially "shorts" [pistols, revolvers] which were always in demand.

'They [the drivers] weren't just from the north or south of Ireland. Some of the lorry drivers were Scots, who supported the IRA. There were also seamen who went off the ship and picked up gear. Drivers could also say what British army units were coming in and leaving. Any intelligence was useful. Long-distance drivers were invaluable. Some guys were travelling two or three times a week. Some drivers would have carried anything or done anything.

we knew everything about individuals and locations. I reckon, in the end, though, they were not taken out, not for military reasons but for political reasons' – the IRA was running down the campaign towards a ceasefire and did not want to be accused of killing Protestants or to provoke retaliation from the UVF, which could spiral into a series of tit-for-tat killings. It is equally possible, however, that if RUC Special Branch were so careful about protecting their agent from other RUC investigators, they would use whatever information they had from informers in the IRA to ensure that operations directed against UVF killers would fail.

North Belfast was not the only location where Bradley's information from 'The Jew' was not used. 'There was this club in the Donegall Road where all the Red Hand Commando in Belfast were being sworn in. We had a "buster" about it in 1992, but Gerry Kelly wouldn't allow any action. He wouldn't agree.' An indication of the pressure from surveillance was that during the 'buster' about the club, in Gerry Kelly's house in the Whiterock Road district, no one *spoke* about the proposed operation – they just wrote notes to each other, which were then destroyed.

The 'club' in question was really a squalid, dilapidated band hall off Meridi Street in the loyalist Village district of south Belfast, where the Pride of the Village flute band drilled and practised. The place doubled as an illegal drinking den where drugs were also sold. It was exactly the sort of activity that disgusted Bradley's informant. In April 1994, two years after the IRA's decision not to attack the club, one of the most dreadful murders of the Troubles took place in it. A woman, Margaret Wright, was beaten to death with pool cues in the hall because the drinkers thought she was a Catholic. In fact, she was a Protestant from a loyalist district in west Belfast. The UVF subsequently killed two men they held responsible for the death of Margaret Wright, including the leader of the Red Hand Commando in the Donegall Road area. In this instance, the information Bradley's informant had supplied was never put to use by the IRA.

Another issue that bewildered Bradley was the latitude afforded the UDA's infamous Johnny Adair in the early nineties. Adair led a gang in the lower Shankill district, the so-called C company, which was involved in drug-dealing, prostitution, racketeering and sectarian killings. 'I can't understand why the IRA didn't whack Adair, except for internal political reasons. I was told they [the IRA in Ardoyne] had taken at least a dozen cars over a period of time to go and whack him. I was annoyed. I said to the guy who told me, "That's a dozen houses we've lost for nothing" [meaning the occupants of those houses where cars had been taken were unlikely to support any future IRA operation].

'Nobody put their mind to it. They kept going into the Shankill to do him, but decided it was too risky because the cops were watching Adair. Why didn't they wait for him to come out? How was he let away with what he was doing? The only thing I can think of is he was useful as a bogeyman – helped to keep people hyped up so the IRA could say they were defending the district. People would say, "Oh, Johnny Adair was in the New Lodge yesterday driving around – oh, oh, scary, you know?" We could easily have done him. How was he not? When you think of what the IRA was capable of. Take the Night of the Long Knives.' This is a reference to Hallow-een 1992 when the IRA in Belfast eliminated the so-called Irish People's Liberation Organisation (IPLO), an offshoot of the INLA, based in the Falls district; it was, in fact, a front for drug-dealing and extortion. The operation was timed to coincide with Hallow-een when the sound of gunfire could not be distinguished from bangers and other fireworks going off. It involved over sixty IRA men. One IPLO man was shot dead in a club in the Short Strand district and ten others in west Belfast were wounded.

'The IPLO was threatening IRA volunteers. The IPLO were criminals, drug-dealers. They were starting to take on 'RA men, confront them. The civil administration could do nothing about them. The operation that night was huge. There was intelligence gathered for weeks about where they were and where they were drinking. It was all to be done in one night. In fact, it took two nights. Loads of the IPLO were kneecapped with AKs. Serious stuff. Your leg's ruined. Most of the IPLO, in fact, gave information and made deals to avoid being kneecapped. The IRA closed down the IPLO in two days. It all involved a huge amount of intelligence and profiling. Local 'RA men thought there was nothing going to be done about the carry-on of the IPLO until that night, then sud-denly it was all over. Now, are you telling me that they couldn't have dealt with the likes of Johnny Adair? There was some reason they decided not to. It was a disgrace.'

To a large extent, however, Bradley was a spectator in the day-to-day affairs of the Belfast Brigade in the years 1990-93. As he says, he was working for GHQ. What he was doing was raising funds for the IRA, mainly through robberies and hijackings. According to the RUC's Detective Chief Superintendent Derek Martindale, in May 1992 the IRA needed running expenses amounting to £7 million a year. Martindale was to cross Bradley's path two years later, but in 1992 they had heard of each other only by repute. Bradley says, 'The IRA needed money all the time for weapons, ammo, to pay volunteers, for prisoners' families – and there were still plenty of them – and for the families of dead volunteers. It may only have been £10 or £20 a week each, but added together it was a lot of money, never mind the gear.'

Bradley regarded his fund-raising as primarily for the IRA, whereas by the early nineties the money was also pouring into Sinn Féin to bankroll offices, election posters, glossy pamphlets, all the paraphernalia of a large and successful political party, but a party that, in 1992, had no paid elected representatives, Gerry Adams having lost his West Belfast seat in that year's general election. Other parties repeatedly questioned how Sinn Féin could afford such extravagant electioneering. The answer was the money Bradley's squad raised. Ten years later, in 2002, the House of Commons Northern Ireland Affairs Committee estimated the IRA's running costs at £1.5 million a year, much reduced from a decade earlier when the military campaign was in operation. The committee estimated the IRA's fund-raising capacity remained at between £5 million and £8 million a year. The surplus went to Sinn Féin.

For Gerry Bradley, now approaching forty but as active as ever, the period from the end of the eighties until 1994 was the most productive, successful and personally satisfying in his IRA career because he was largely in control of what he was doing. He attended 'busters' and was still, even at his age, prepared to take part in operations, apparently as normal. Apart from a couple of very senior IRA men, no one knew that Bradley and another man called 'Conker' were running a special squad that was primarily responsible in the North for raising funds for the IRA. To all intents and purposes, the squad was operating an IRA franchise all over Ireland, with as free a hand as he could have wished. He reported only to one member of GHQ staff, the Director of Intelligence, whom he calls 'Duckser'.

The squad operated from Belfast to Derry to south Armagh and all points in between. 'We picked our own men, we did not go through the normal IRA channels. Only two senior IRA men outside the squad knew about it. We were responsible for getting our own "gear", from guns right down to hoods and gloves. We had a float of £300 to £400 for that – also, in case you needed taxis or anything. Conker ran the squad's ops on a day-to-day basis. He was brilliant at it. We were working from 8.00am to 10.00pm, planning, doing hijackings, robberies, stacking stuff away, selling it on.'

Bradley met members of the squad about once a week in houses in west or north Belfast, never in bars or in the centre of the city. He met the IRA's Director of Intelligence, to whom he reported, two or three times a week in restaurants or cafés.

'The squad did not socialise together and we never met publicly. Everyone was trusted and no one was caught. We had our own transport, our own warehouse on the Shore Road, where you'd least expect it to be [being a predominantly loyalist area]. You could take a forty-footer that we'd hijacked into the warehouse, change its plates, sell its contents. We were doing ops continuously all over the place. We even did an op in Boucher Road [a two-mile-long strip of warehouses, depots, car-showrooms, up-market furniture shops, bathroom and kitchen-appliance shops] which was nearly impossible to get into, it was that full of cops and undercover men. When OC Belfast found out we'd done it, he was annoyed. He said if he'd known he'd have got us to bring in a "smokey" [bomb]. The only reason he found out was in case we got our wires crossed with some other squad operating in Belfast trying to get into Boucher Road, and even then he only knew me and Conker of the squad.'

Bradley had no compunction about carrying out those activities. Fund-raising by expropriation was all part of the IRA campaign against the British. If he managed to scare off investment, undermine confidence, damage the North's economy, so much the better. Was that not what the IRA was supposed to be about: destroying the local economy in order to undermine the so-called state? He firmly believed that Northern Ireland had no legitimacy or credibility as a state. Anything he could do to damage it, maintain instability, cost the British Exchequer money, Bradley would do.

Years after the arrest of Bradley's squad, the IRA was still carrying out the same kind of operations, culminating in the colossal robbery of £37million and an unknown amount of foreign currency from the Northern Bank headquarters in Belfast in December 2004, ten years after the first ceasefire in 1994. Amazingly, until the Northern bank robbery, the British and Irish governments turned a blind eye to these activities, not wishing to upset political progress. In January 2005, the then Taoiseach, Bertie Ahern, told the Dáil: 'This was tolerated in order to try to move the process forward. However, ten years on [after the ceasefire], we cannot continue to do that.' Astonishingly, he went on, 'I did not show anger regarding earlier events', and then listed heists in 2004 in Belfast and in Strabane totalling several million pounds. 'We, in this House, took that coolly enough,' he said. The Northern Bank robbery was the last straw.

In the years immediately before the 1994 ceasefire, the squad robbed bookies of money, warehouses of cigarettes, electrical goods and white goods, hijacked lorry-loads of tobacco and alcohol, and produced money from every conceivable source all over the North. Bradley rejects the term 'extortion' because of its association with criminality. 'Extortion is what loyalists did. We were handing the money over to the army. It was to fund the war: it wasn't for us personally. We were as poor at the end of it all as we were at the start.

'Often a phone-call was enough for people, say, from bingo halls or pubs, to fill a briefcase with money: you didn't have to go in with guns or anything. We also did "handovers": that's where the security man or somebody on the inside just gave us the money and said they'd been robbed by men in balaclavas with guns. We tried to build up a network of contacts willing to buy. Cigarettes was the big thing. Everyone wanted to buy them; then booze, clothes, electrics. We had guys in the Post Office who would tell us when money was being moved. They tipped us off about codes and wrappers on bags and bundles. They told us different colours of labels represented money – that sort of thing. We had contacts in banks and hospitals. We thought about getting into art and antiques. We learned that there was always a buyer. We had a network stretching to London.'

Sometimes the owners of premises would approach the IRA and ask for their place to be bombed or burnt, offering a cut of the compensation money. One such occasion almost resulted in the death of both Bradley and Conker. The owner of a large pub with function rooms offered £20,000 if the IRA would destroy his property. Duckser estimated that wrecking it would need a 500kg bomb, which would be too much hassle. He asked Bradley to have a look at the place, which he did. Bradley then went to Terry McIvor, the IRA's veteran electronics-cum-explosives expert, and told him the layout of the place. McIvor reckoned the job could be done without explosives. His plan was to cover electric fires in a function room with rags, douse the place with petrol, turn on all gas appliances and then set a timer for the electric fires to come on once everyone had left the premises.

When the electric fires had heated up they would set the rags on fire, which in turn would ignite the petrol fumes and combine with the gas to cause an almighty explosion, wrecking the place. The plan had many attractions, not least the fact that there was no need to risk transporting a huge bomb. Indeed, there was no need to transport anything except the timer for the electric fire socket, which could be bought in Boots or Argos.

McIvor's plan was duly carried out. Bradley and Conker went to the bar, where they sat for an hour or so, ostensibly out for a drink. After all other customers had left, the pair went to the toilets, pulled on hoods, came out and tied up and blindfolded the last two staff in the building. They went out to the carpark, donned gloves and boiler suits, then returned and set about pouring petrol and turning on gas: Conker set the timer and plugged it in. Bradley was ushering the blindfolded staff out along a corridor when there was an enormous 'whoomp' and a ball of fire came billowing down the corridor. Bradley threw both staff down and lay on them as the whoosh of flame roared over them. Bradley says, 'It was like *Backdraft*, that film with Kurt Russell in it.' Miraculously, they were all unharmed. The only casualties were Bradley's eyebrows, singed off. He and Conker got the staff out into the carpark and drove off, tyres squealing, still wearing their boiler suits, which were reeking of petrol. Their last sight was of the windows blowing out as a series of gas explosions ripped the place apart, while the two staff, still bound and blindfolded, blundered about the carpark.

In the gloom in the function room, Conker had set the timer wrongly, perhaps mistaking ten-second divisions on the dial for minutes. The electric fires must have come on almost immediately, lighting the rags and commencing the process of destruction. By the normal laws of physics, they should all have been killed. When they reported to Duckser, Conker 'thought Bradley deserved a bit of credit for his efforts in getting the staff out from the blazing pub, but all Duckser was interested in was knowing when was the next op.'

At the height of the squad's success and against his better judgement, Bradley agreed to participate in an operation he did not like the sound of and which turned out to have been compromised before it began. It was an old-fashioned assassination attempt against a senior police officer, the sort of operation that had never been done successfully in Belfast even at the height of the IRA campaign, let alone in its dog days. Out of the blue, one day in January 1994, 'Duckser says, "Who wants to fire an AK?" One of the guys, Cheeser, was always saying at busters, "Where's the AKs?" Now he was on the spot, could hardly back off. So, of course he said he wanted to. But he was a lifer out on licence, and lifers were not supposed to be in ASUs because if they were caught they had to do the rest of their life sentence as well as the new one. I tried to keep him at the back of things, but he was that keen. Duckser told me, "I don't want you in this", that is out in the actual op, but he wanted me setting it up.

'It was a major op. The plan was to whack Martindale [Chief Superintendent Derek Martindale] as he was driven on his regular route into Belfast in the morning. Why Martindale? Well, he was in charge of all the informers – ran them; he was Special Branch. I suppose, too, it was a "big hit", to say: we can hit anybody, any time, any place. The hit was to be in east Belfast, a huge risk, big problems for the run back – but where else could you do him?'

In fact, Martindale was not Special Branch but a senior CID officer, who had led C-13, the RUC's anti-racketeering unit, which, ironically, would have had Gerry Bradley's squad in its sights in 1992 and 1993 as the RUC sought to crack down on IRA fund-raising. In May 1992, C-13 executed 'Operation Crystal', the largest ever drive against IRA fund-raising. They deployed thousands of soldiers and police in high-profile raids in south Down and south Armagh, where they seized piles of documents and computer equipment as well as confiscating tens of thousands of pounds worth of CDs, videos and counterfeit goods. The exercise was a failure in that it did not bring any of the main IRA finance operations to an end or convict any senior operators. However, it did, for a while, seriously disrupt IRA activities relating to bars, clubs, businesses and smuggling in those counties, though it also disclosed the extent of police intelligence about those affairs. It also brought Martindale to public prominence as he gave interviews about the operation and commented on the extent and nature of IRA financing. Perhaps IRA GHQ had decided to hit back at Martindale before any ceasefire prevented them settling old scores?

In January 1994, Gerry Adams and Martin McGuinness, and their supporters on the Army Council, were bringing round the rest of the IRA leadership to declaring a ceasefire. They were under enormous political pressure to do so. The Taoiseach, Albert Reynolds, and the British Prime Minister, John Major, had publicly subscribed to a document called 'The Downing Street Declaration', standing before the Downing Street Christmas tree in December 1993. The declaration had contained language and phrases previously agreed with the IRA leadership which both Irish and British governments believed would result in a ceasefire, but there was no sign of one.

Instead, Sinn Féin requested clarification of a number of items in the declaration, while the IRA continued into 1994 with shooting and rocket and bomb attacks on the security forces. Later in the year, they embarked on a series of killings of senior loyalists, which looked like paying off old scores. The attack on Chief Superintendent Martindale fits with this tactic. Martindale had survived an IRA attack about ten years earlier in Derry, and clearly remained a prime target for the IRA leadership.

Bradley becomes very angry and resentful as he recalls the chaos, stupidity and disorganisation surrounding the attack on Martindale. He still wonders about the logic of taking members of the successful squad he was in and using them for the operation. Duckser assured Bradley and Cheeser that 'no one else knows about the op'. IRA intelligence had noted that Martindale was a creature of habit. He came into work every day at the same time along the same route from his home in the north Down suburbs of Belfast.

The plan was to rent a flat in the Belmont area of east Belfast. The hit team would stay overnight in the flat, then come out in the morning, get into a van left outside for them and drive to the spot where they would carry out the attack on Martindale's car. The key ingredient was surprise.

Bradley met Duckser in Frames snooker hall near Unity Flats, where Duckser was going through adverts in the *Belfast Telegraph* for flats in Belmont. Bradley had a mobile phone that had been supplied by Peter Keeley, an IRA man from Newry who had been in Belfast for some months. Unfortunately for the operation, Keeley was also a Special Branch informer, who later went by the name Kevin Fulton. It was the first time a mobile had ever been used in an IRA operation in Belfast. There is no doubt the phone was carefully monitored by the police and its whereabouts tracked at all times.

Bradley says: 'Keeley came across as a wheeler-dealer, a fly boy. He was all into sharp clothes, flash cars. He was a "Del boy" – gave the impression he could get anything, fix anything. He always had a mobile phone. Nobody had a mobile in those days. He hung around, made himself useful, supplied stuff.

'In those days, using a mobile was like putting a brick to your ear, they were that big. Nothing would do Duckser but he would use the mobile to phone about the flat in Belmont. I said to him, "Don't be using that mobile." I pointed out a pay phone on the wall ten feet way, but no, he had to use the mobile.

'He asked me to get the flat organised. I got a girl to go to rent it out. I gave her strict forensic instructions. Like: wear gloves; don't take them off under any circumstances – even if you have to go to the toilet, don't take them off. She was brilliant. The landlord asked her for ID. She had none. He said he needed references. She had no references. Then, what about her work address? She told him he couldn't contact her work. She just flirted outrageously with the guy, told him she was living with her sister and her husband, and they wanted her out. She really needed the flat asap. She let him think he could jump her as soon as she moved in. He took the bait and she got it.'

As the day for the operation approached, there were more and more indications that it was compromised. Three or four days before the attack, Bradley was to meet someone in the New Lodge. One of the best places was at Artillery House, out of sight of the surveillance equipment in the army sangar on Templar House. Bradley drove to the spot, and as he stopped he noticed a man in a car looking at him. He suspected it was an undercover man. Bradley pretended to fiddle with stuff in his car while the other man got out of his car. The man went into a shop at the corner of the street. Bradley said to himself: 'If this guy turns or looks at me when he comes out of the shop, I'm gonna go for him. In fact, he must have thrown his money on the counter and taken a paper because he was out so fast. He immediately turns to look where I am and I ran at him. He bolted, jumped into his car and made off.'

Meanwhile, Duckser told Bradley another member of the squad, who had not been in it too long, had been 'gripped' in the Cliftonville district, and Special Branch had asked him to work undercover, to pass information. If that was not bad enough, plain-clothes detectives had walked into the workplace of the girl-friend of a third member of the team, Davy Adams, and told her

Davy was going to get into trouble. Bradley says: 'Duckser asked me, "Whaddya reckon?" I said, "They're telling us, they're warning us, don't try this. We're going to do youse." I told Duckser they were all over us. The whole op stank. I told him about chasing the guy in the New Lodge and he said, "Why did you do that?" What a question. What was I supposed to do, let him think I hadn't noticed?

'The night before the operation, Davy Adams and Cheeser went over to the flat. The gear was already there: AKs, a short, blast bomb and so on. There were no lights in the flat. The electricity hadn't been turned on because, of course, the girl hadn't registered. They had got another mobile to keep in contact since everything else was dead.'

In the meantime, Bradley had organised a van in the New Lodge and two men took over the house from which the van was to be taken. Duckser and Bradley waited for the IRA driver, who was due to come from west Belfast, but there was no sign of him. Half an hour went by, then an hour. 'I'm saying to Duckser, over and over, "Where is this guy, where's the guy that's driving the van?" Duckser actually said, "He's a million percent. Look, if he doesn't turn up you can shoot me!" He didn't turn up.'

In the end, Bradley, who was not supposed to be involved in the actual operation, had to drive the van over to Belmont. His nerves were jangling. Too many things were going wrong. As he drove down Donegall Street towards the city centre, soldiers were just setting up a road check. Thirty seconds later and he would have been stopped, van and all – with his known face and no explanation or documents for the vehicle. He left the van at the Belmont flat as arranged, but since his driving the van had been a last minute decision, he had no transport back. He had to walk down the loyalist Newtownards Road, one of the most dangerous districts in the North of Ireland for an IRA man. Finally, at the republican Short Strand, he got a taxi to the New Lodge and went to the house the IRA had taken over.

The woman of the house was deeply resentful and was protesting loudly. The usual IRA procedure would have been to take the occupants away to another location so that they would be in no danger, but also so that they could give only minimal information to police later. Out of the house, they could not make a nuisance of themselves and the IRA operators could have a free hand and, if necessary, develop their own explanation about their presence in the house if the security forces arrived. None of that happened. Bradley did not have enough manpower at his disposal. He would have had to bring in men from another squad, which he did not want to do. He wanted to keep it 'tight'. The people stayed and Bradley and another man, Paddy Donaghy, spent the night there with the occupants and, as he says, 'with a bad, bad feeling. Everything was bad.'

'Next morning the chopper was up, first thing. Something was wrong. My instinct was to get out. But if I did, then maybe the people in the house would phone the police. I just sat there, waiting for the phone call from Belmont to say everything was okay and then

I could get out. Instead, there was a call from somebody saying he was a workmate of the man of the house and wondering why he wasn't at work. I made up some yarn, but the call was to check who would answer the phone in the house. A few minutes after the phone call, I saw the cops coming running: E4A [a highly trained Special Branch unit], Heckler and Koch sub-machine guns – you know, with the flashlight attached – body armour, the whole thing.

'We tore off the hoods and gloves and so on, and stuffed them anywhere and everywhere – under cushions, into drawers – then they crashed in on us. The woman of the house was shouting from upstairs, "Where were youse, last night? The bastards are down there." Then, "It was the wee one, the wee one", meaning me. They tied us up with the white plastic strips, trussed us up like chickens, all the time asking "What are you doing here? Why are you here?" They were really hyped up. The guy who tied me up dragged me out to the kitchen towards the back door. Another cop out in the yard said, "There's a padlock." I reckoned they were gonna do me in the entry, but they couldn't get out through the yard door. The first guy threw me on the ground and stuck his rifle in my mouth, yelling, "Stop staring at me, stop looking at me or I'll kill you", but I just kept looking at him. I knew then he was going to hurt me.'

Bradley and Paddy Donaghy were badly beaten and then carted off to Castlereagh – in Bradley's case, for the last of more than fifty times, he reckons, in his IRA career. His war was over.

After he has been 'processed' in Castlereagh, one of the arrest team came to have a look at Bradley. 'I was in one of those white forensic suits, you know like a spaceman? This guy comes in and stands looking at me. We looked at each other. I says to him, "Youse are good." He says, "Youse are not so bad yourselves."

'During interrogation the cops said, "We've been waiting weeks for youse." They were watching and waiting so long they could have made a film of it.' The whole operation had been a fiasco from start to finish. The police were waiting for the men from the flat at Belmont. No doubt, they had been under surveillance all night. The police knew when and where the attack was to take place, and were ready. Martindale had switched to an armour-plated saloon car the day before. Lying on the floor in the back of his car on the day of the operation was a member of the RUC's SAS-trained Headquarters Mobile Support Unit, armed with a Heckler and Koch G3 rifle. Travelling behind Martindale's car was a dingy Ford Transit van, with ladders and piping tied to its roof rack, but with a powerfully tuned engine under the bonnet. Inside was a HMSU squad with massive firepower.

When the IRA squad in their van drove out of Belmont Avenue at 7.00am in front of Martindale's car, his police driver was expecting them. He swung away and the Ford Transit behind accelerated to cut in front of the IRA's van. Cheeser and Davy Adams jumped out and ran for it, but they were quickly overwhelmed by heavily-armed police coming from all directions. They were savagely beaten by police and by public-spirited passers-by, who joined in the hammering of the IRA men. The police continued to assault the IRA men after their arrest. Davy Adams ended up in intensive prevents employers taking them on, or they may have to sign a form asking if they have any criminal convictions. Republican former prisoners refuse to sign such a form because they insist their convictions were political, not criminal offences. After all, they were released under the terms of the Good Friday Agreement, a political arrangement that waived sentence time.

More than half of the twenty-seven Sinn Féin Stormont assembly members elected in 2007 are former prisoners, as are two of Sinn Féin's TDs. Thus, there is the bizarre situation where a former prisoner can be a minister in the northern executive or sit in a national parliament, but most formal employment is closed to them. Until a few years ago, they could not even drive a taxi in the North because they could not obtain a public service vehicle (PSV) licence. In 2003, Sean Crowe TD, speaking in the Dáil on the Taxi Regulation Bill asked the then Transport Minister, the late Seamus Brennan, if former IRA prisoners could be exempt from restrictions on driving taxis. Brennan turned down his request without a vote: they must go to the district court and plead their case. Yet many former prisoners are now in their fifties facing the prospect of living on state benefits, since they have not been able to build up a pension. The widespread unemployment among former prisoners impoverishes their families, who are also forced to live on benefits.

So far, there is no indication that any of these circumstances will improve. Although Sinn Féin is in power in the North's administration, they have shown little inclination to exert any pressure on behalf of former IRA prisoners. In any case, the political reality is that unionists would be so completely opposed to any efforts to improve the lot of republican ex-prisoners that Sinn Féin may have decided it is too soon to try.

For former IRA members, the outcome of their war is far from what they hoped when they joined all those years ago.

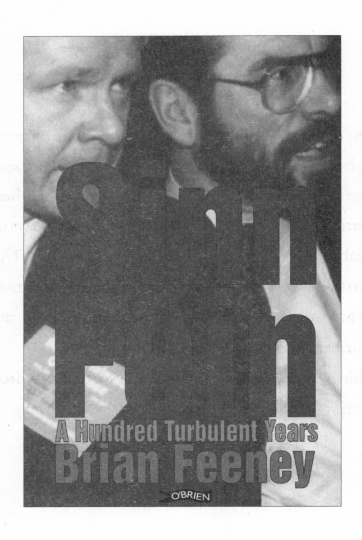

OTHER BOOKS FROM THE O'BRIEN PRESS

FROM BRIAN FEENEY

The definitive account of the history of Sinn Féin from its beginnings to today. The complete story of a party that repeatedly reshaped its identity over a hundred years, moving from dual monarchy in the early days to dual strategy – the armalite and the ballot box. The party that sometimes took on the non-participation stance to becoming one of the leading parties in the Northern Assembly.

This is an amazing story of a momentous hundred years, told in detail, and with authority, by Feeney.

O'BRIEN POCKET HISTORY OF

The Troubles

UPDATED EDITION

Brian Feeney

OTHER BOOKS FROM THE O'BRIEN PRESS

FROM BRIAN FEENEY

From the Divis Street riots of 1964 to the tortuous political manoeuvrings that culminated in the 2007 Assembly elections, this book traces the reality of life in Northern Ireland during the Troubles. It explains the origins of the Civil Rights movement, the motivation behind the IRA's armed struggle, the murder campaigns of various Loyalist terror groups, the major incidents of violence, and the response of the British security forces and the judicial system. It describes what it was like to live with bombs, army searches in the dead of night, death threats to politicians, activists and others. A concise yet detailed account of the political and personal toll of the Northern Ireland conflict.

OTHER BOOKS FROM THE O'BRIEN PRESS

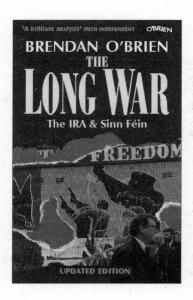

'A brilliant analysis of how Sinn Féin/IRA have moved from the negative theology of the Ó Brádaigh years to the positive political activism of the Adams-McGuinness leadership.'
Irish Independent

'From a well-informed, fair-minded observer, a courageous book, with much news to tell ... Brendan O'Brien knows just about everything about the Provisional IRA ... a crisp and uncensorious account'
Mail on Sunday

OTHER BOOKS FROM THE O'BRIEN PRESS

A political history of the SDLP and Sinn Féin from the onset of the Troubles to the present day. This book outlines the ideological and electoral rivalry between the two parties and assesses the contribution of each to the reshaping of modern nationalist politics in Nothern Ireland.

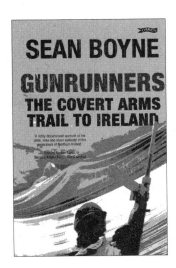

The true, gripping story of how paramilitaries smuggled arms into Ireland during the Troubles. This deadly trade involved international intrigue, shadowy arms dealers, spy satellites, stings, moles and murder.

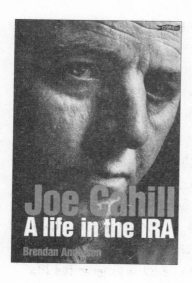

From one of the best-known and most admired lifelong IRA members, a unique inside story, as told to Brendan Anderson, revealing the workings of this paramilitary organisation over the past sixty years, as well as his own commitment and activites.

Forthright and outspoken, this is a unique first-hand account of a most exciting and important period in Irish history from one who was deeply involved. Wife, mother, revolutionary, politician, widow, Lord Mayor of Dublin, Clarke tells the inside story of the 1916 Rising which she helped to plan with her husband, Tom Clarke, who was executed after the Rising.

OTHER BOOKS FROM THE O'BRIEN PRESS

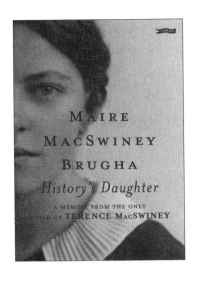

A deeply personal memoir, with wonderful photos and mementos, from the daughter of Terence McSwiney. McSwiney died on hunger strike in Brixton Jail, and his body was brought back to Cork, where he had been Lord Mayor, for a huge funeral. His daughter was raised in Germany and later married the son of Cathal Brugha, who also gave his life for Irish freedom.

In 1918 Éamon de Valera arrived in America using the title: President of Ireland. He spent eighteen months publicising his nation's plight and raising millions of dollars for the cause of Irish independence. His was a remarkable journey where every step came freighted with political intrigue, personal vendettas, spying, propaganda wars and assassination plots.

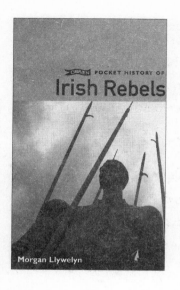

The lives and deeds of Irish rebels such as Granuaile, Wolfe Tone, Robert Emmet, Daniel O'Connell, James Connolly, Constance Markievicz, Patrick Pearse, Bobby Sands, Gerry Addams ... and others.

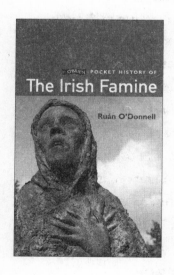

An overview of the economic and social contexts that contributed to the Irish Famine. The book explains why so many were dependent on the potato, addresses disagreements between political leaders, and controversial distribution of what little food was available. Includes first-hand accounts of awful conditions, of ruthless evictions, suffering in workhouses and aboard 'coffin ships'.

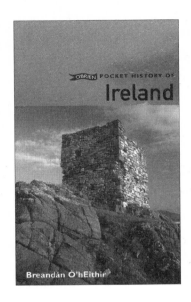

The story of Ireland from pre-history to the twentieth century from an author well known for his entertaining take on the country and its controversial history.

'A valuable guide to Irish history' *Irish Echo*

'Of great interest and practical use for readers from Ireland or abroad' *Leinster Leader*

A magnificently illustrated history for all ages, full of fascinating details.

It begins after the Ice Age and chronicles invasions, wars, Christianity, famine, a divided island; it also includes tales of Celtic head hunters, mysterious stone tombs, the Viking Ivar the Boneless, the Black Death, life in castles, superstitions, schools, games, the *Titanic* tragedy, music, mobiles and computers.

Filled with historical images, maps, population trees, and fun.